A WINDOW ON SOWETO

by

Joyce Sikakane

International Defence & Aid Fund
104 Newgate Street, London EC1
June 1977

ISBN No. 0 904759 17 2

Contents

Life in Soweto

Life in Soweto starts at about 4 a.m. Mind you Soweto is never sleepy. There is the in and out movement of workers who do shift work. The sonorous roar of fast-moving trains running in and out every minute to collect workers is heard from 4 am. and dies out just after midnight.

Imagine, at the crack of dawn, the haze of greyish-brown smoke enshrouding the ghetto. It indicates that inside the matchbox houses the inmates have woken up. The one whose turn it is—be it father, mother, daughter or son—jumps out of the blankets first to light the coal-stove, and thus the smoke belches from each chimney engulfing the ghetto. A figure of a girl, usually from the six to ten-year-olds, emerges from the sleeping spot. The girl is on tip-toe gently holding a chamberpot lest it spill on someone's feet or the floor. Near the door she carefully puts it on the floor, opens the door, picks up the pot and puts it down on the ground outside and quickly shuts the door. She picks up the pot and rushes to empty it in the lavatory. Once outside drops of urine falling on the ground do not call for retribution. Because the boys, fathers and uncles hate using the potty at night, they are the first to unbolt the back-door and scurry, in turns, to the loo.

Those families whose stoves have hot-water boilers do not have to wait long for washing water, because the overnight coal fire keeps the water hot. Otherwise it means that the one whose turn it is has to wake up an hour earlier, to empty the ash, lay the paper, wood and coal and make a fire. Then fill up a big pot with cold water. The hot water ready, each member of the family in turn takes a sponge in a galvanized tub standing on a bench in one corner of a room. After each wash, the soiled water is thrown down the only drainage attached to the toilet wall.

Meanwhile, at the stove, the one on duty cooks soft mealie meal porridge in a huge pot. The sound of the hissing kettle, ready for the mugs of tea and coffee, breaks the dreariness inside the house. In the dining-room/sitting-room converted to a bedroom at night, in the only bedroom and kitchen itself, someone is folding the double-bed sofa, making up the beds or rolling the sleeping mats. Others are dressing, combing their hair and, in the case of the women, applying their face-cream. After dressing the next point is the stove, where, in turn, each member pours porridge into a bowl, quickly cools it and nimbles it down the throat. To add milk to the porridge is a luxury, let alone eating a slice of brown bread spread with margarine or peanut butter.

The men feel the inside pocket of their jackets, just to make sure that the 'stinker' or pass book is safely tucked in or else it means being picked up by the police. The women too search their handbags for the 'stinker'; once sure it is

5

there, they brave themselves for the road to the white man's city. All this activity inside the casements is swift, because the machine of the white economy is waiting for black hands to turn its wheels.

The workers then spill out into the dark or dimly-lit streets of Soweto hurrying to the bus terminii, the taxi ranks and railway stations. It is very rare for any worker to board a bus, a taxi or a train without having stumbled across a corpse lying in a street. It is agony for a family to see day-break with one member having not slept at home. Immediately one of them is assigned to go and look for the missing person. Should members of such a family reach their point of departure to work, without recognizing one of the dead bodies they saw lying in the streets, they sigh with relief. But fear soon grips the search party should the missing person not be found at a police station or hospital. The last resort is to inspect the corpses in the government mortuary. Wails greet the body on being discovered in the morgue. The search is done at a sacrifice, jobwise, because invariably the employers are not sympathetic to absenteeism.

Travelling to the city is largely done by rail. There are approximately 13 stations on the two-track railway line in this vast labour reservoir. The main junction connecting the rail link with the other West Rand locations is New Canada station, five miles from the ghetto towards the city.

There are 411 trains running in and out of Soweto and Johannesburg daily, carrying over 200,000 passengers in one direction each day. The trains have 11 coaches each, two of which have cushioned seats and are supposedly reserved as first-class, and the rest are for what is termed 'third-class' passengers. There is a shortage of room in these coaches. Sometimes, when the train driver is out of proper gear as the train pulls into a station, the first-class coaches (which are immediately behind the engine) happen to be nearer to the 'other' passengers, whose coaches lag behind the platform. Rather than risk being late for work, passengers jump in indiscriminately. Soweto trains are notorious for their intolerance in waiting for passengers to get out or jump in.

According to a newspaper report, Mr. Jack Lloyd, a planning engineer for the South African Railways, caused railway enthusiasts and transport experts to gasp when he revealed how crowded Soweto's trains actually were. Addressing members of the Railway Society of Southern Africa in Johannesburg, Mr. Lloyd illustrated his point by explaining that the SAR was having problems with damage to the battery boxes which are suspended beneath the coaches. "We couldn't understand what was causing it," he said. "It was only after we had done some tests in the workshop that we realised the coaches were packed so full that the frames were actually sagging under the weight, causing the battery boxes to touch the rails." (*Rand Daily Mail* 14/5/76).

It is the African worker, the poorest paid of all workers, who enables the railways to run at a profit. In one budget speech, the Minister of Transport boasted that passenger traffic had increased rail earnings because of the amount spent by the "Bantu" third class. Main line earnings showed an advance of 13·4 per cent in 1969/70.

There are regular accidents on these trains, often involving terrible loss of life or limb. It seems that safety is ignored if the passengers are black.

Because of the unsafe condition of the trains and the reckless way they are driven, there are frequent accidents on these trains. In the eyes of the Soweto community such accidents are interpreted as deliberate slaughter of the African people. Such inferences are made because the white drivers always seem to escape uninjured leaving a mass of African bodies crushed into unrecognition and hundreds more maimed for life. In the late 1960's Cecilia Masondo, wife of a longterm Robben Island prisoner, had her leg amputated after an accident. She never fully recovered from the shock.

Those survivors and relatives who submitted claims against South African Railways fought a losing battle, for SAR would offer to settle out of court through the Bantu Affairs Commissioner not a third party of the claimants' choice. And the "stinker" was all important: no claim could be made without one, but who collected the passes from the bodies? The SAR police. Nor did the police ever take the initiative of informing relatives, it was up to them to report a missing person. If a person dead or injured was in Soweto "illegally" no compensation could be claimed. So it took the most militant relatives armed with undisputed evidence to claim and win. When successful compensation was paid it was not as a lump sum but in long term instalments.

Then there is the "tsotsi" (gangster) element which picks pockets, so that a number of workers reach home minus a weekly or monthly pay-packet. Because passengers have to push their way in and out of the trains, women lose their handbags, scarves and shoes. Those who wear spectacles run the hazard of glasses breaking on their faces because of pushing elbows. Paperbags stuffed with food and clothing bought on payday are held tightly to the owner's bosom lest they get accidentally strewn amongst the rushing crowds.

There is the Putco bus service which mainly serves the workers who live in Diepkloof, Meadowlands and Dobsonville where there is no railway link. This bus service is as bad as the trains.

A few hundred workers use taxis to travel to work. They are passengers who are hurrying to do overtime work, those who missed their usual train, and those returning home after shopping. Taxi-fares are high, and taxis are few because the Department of Transport issues a quota of licences annually. It is not government policy to encourage African cab-owners in "white" urban areas. The African worker who possesses a car hesitates to drive it to the city because of the fear of a breakdown. Besides, it costs money to park and buy petrol. The worker uses his car on Sunday to visit relatives, attend a wedding or a funeral.

As soon as the black workers arrive in the white city, the routes which they take get coloured black, until every worker disappears into the buildings where they toil. The return to Soweto starts at 4 p.m. reaching its peak between 5 p.m and 7 p.m. and goes on steadily until just after midnight.

Housing in Soweto

Soweto (jocularly called by its inhabitants "so-where-to") is the largest single modern ghetto in Africa. Soweto is a bastard child born out of circumstances following the dispossession of the African people and the discovery of gold in the Witwatersrand. It was born out of white greed and racism perpetrated against the Africans. Even its name is a bastard one, taken from its geographical location: **South West Townships**.

There are 26 locations which cover 85 square kilometres. The 108,766 red or grey brick houses with multi-coloured roofs that make up the smog-smothered ghetto are built opposite each other in straight single rows running parallel to a street. A common feature of the huge settlement is that fifty yards from each house is a backyard toilet separated by a wall from that of a neighbour's. Naked bulbs hanging on roughly installed electric cables cast a dim light inside some of the houses. Most homes use candles, paraffin or gas lamps for lighting. Coal stoves are used in almost all the homes.

Standard four-roomed Soweto house.

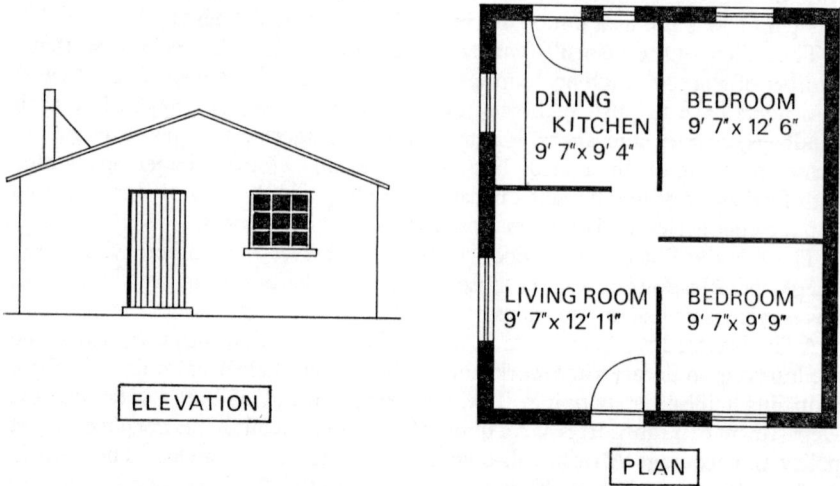

ELEVATION

DINING KITCHEN 9' 7"x 9' 4"

BEDROOM 9' 7"x 12' 6"

LIVING ROOM 9' 7"x 12' 11"

BEDROOM 9' 7"x 9' 9"

PLAN

The sizes of the houses vary. Some of the very first built locations consist of two or three tiny rooms with small verandahs. Their only water supply is through a tap attached to one of the walls of the backyard toilet. Then there are the army barrack shaped ones—three to four rooms, without bathrooms, but with a tap

8

hanging outside each back wall. The four to five roomed houses of Orlando West are an exception to other four-roomed houses forming 98 per cent of the Soweto complex. These houses are exclusive in that each has an indoor shower room with a tap. Some are also provided with a kitchen sink or pantry. Scattered here and there in Soweto are a variety of small three-roomed enclaves whose walls, floors and roofs are all made of concrete blocks.

An average of six to seven people occupy Soweto homes of less than four rooms and four of these people being adults.

Only a quarter of the houses in Soweto have running cold water inside the houses. In all the others, residents fetch cold water by buckets from the outside taps. Only three in every hundred houses have running hot water. Only seven in a hundred have a bath or shower. Only fifteen in a hundred houses have electricity.

Situated in the heart of the slum are the attractive lodgings of Soweto's rich class. The select Dube Township, designed and created as a show piece of "African advancement" displays costly palatially-built houses forming a sharp contrast to the multifarious staid matchbox confines surrounding it. The creation of Dube Township in 1955 was a result of a tactical manoeuvre by the government so as to succeed with its segregated housing policy. At the beginning of 1955, Sophiatown, a suburb within the confines of the City in which Africans owned properties, was demolished. In order to succeed in removing African property-owners from Sophiatown the government created Dube Township. Here plots were made available for purchase by the aspiring moneyed Africans.

These undeveloped plots were sold to the buyers on a 90-year lease basis. Purchasers bought plots and constructed stylish houses of their own choice. The township was named after Mr. John Dube one of the first distinguished African educationalists and principal of an African teacher training college in South Africa. Ironically Mr. Dube was also the first President of the African National Congress of South Africa. Residents of this glamorous township are composed of doctors, lawyers, teachers, nurses, highly paid white collar workers and businessmen. The ghetto dwellers generally refer to Dube Township as the home of "Situations" because it is choice situated, or as the place of the "excuse me's" because the African intelligentsia residing there prefer speaking English, or as the suburb of the "highbugs", "tycoons" and "socialites" because some homeowners are businessmen and those who like the glamour of public life.

To the ordinary Sowetonian Dube Township gives a feeling of being out of place because it imposes a false picture of contentment, gaiety and affluence amidst a huge dissatisfied, gloomy, hardworking and poverty-stricken community. White tourists are taken to Dube to see how comfortably the "Bantu" live.

Separately built in some of the 26 locations are the most notorious and depressing barracks known as hostels. There are about a dozen of them. These long narrow-built compartments accommodate "single" men i.e. migrant workers. In Soweto alone 60,000 men are hostel dwellers. Indoors, the inmates share the

9

dormitories in tribal groups, as required by government law. In each dormitory are moveable black-painted iron and steel beds, a common one-plate coal stove and iron bar lockers used by the occupants. Each dormitory has a common cold water shower room. Barbed wire fences divide the hostel premises from that of the locations. There are no dining-rooms, no visitors' rooms, no reading rooms, no recreation facilities, and absolutely no privacy for the inmates. Women are not allowed to venture into the hostel premises. Here in these hostels thousands of African men are caged after working hours.

Most of these "single" male occupants are migrant workers from the Bantustans. They consist of respectable married men forced by migratory laws to leave their wives and children in the homelands, of divorced men and widowers evicted from Soweto houses because they are without spouses. By government law, no single man or woman is allowed to rent a house in Soweto. Some of the men are bachelors from the homelands and from Soweto, the latter being men no longer qualifying to lodge with their parents as they are of working age.

For instance, Dube Hostel, one of the many hostels, houses over 6,000 male migrant workers, only 5 per cent of whom are short-term contract labourers, the other 95 per cent stay indefinitely irrespective of their marital status.

A hostel for single women was built in Mzimhlophe, just a stone's throw from a male one. This hostel houses 800 women. It consists of four-roomed blocks each with a common bathroom. Two occupants share a room. The "single" women inmates are mostly domestic servants, factory workers and office tea-makers. They are women who, during the mass urban removals and resettlements, were found to be without spouses. Some of them are "push-outs" from the Soweto housing system. The latter group are girls of working age—16 years upwards according to the government law which compels African women to carry reference books, and thus if they are not at school should be employed. Widows and divorcees, orphans and unmarried mothers are also included. Mothers are not allowed to reside with their children in the hostels. Men are also forbidden into the hostel premises. No visitors are allowed. The hostel premises are fenced with barbed wire.

Rent for each inmate of these single-sex hostels varies from R7 to R8 a month. These single-sex hostels are hovels for men and women denied the right to lead creative lives.

Some of the houses which have family occupants have small gardens and Sowetonians take a pride in planting flowers and lawns, with a peach or apricot tree here and there. Streets in Soweto are narrow, dusty in winter and full of potholes. They turn into streams during heavy rains in summer. A few of the streets have dim electric lights. Only those leading to police stations, administration offices, bottle stores and the big Johannesburg City are brightly lit. By 1976 Soweto had only 39 public telephones—one for every 25,900 people. The 985 private phones are installed in police stations, administration offices, post offices, shops, doctors' consulting rooms and a few private homes.

History

The history of Soweto has behind it the history of land division in South Africa—the original conflict between the African inhabitants and the European migrants and still today the determining feature of inequality and injustice under apartheid.

Sometime in the 19th century when what is now called the Republic of South Africa was still divided into two British colonies—the Cape of Good Hope and Natal; and the two Boer Republics—the Orange Free State and the Transvaal, the indigenous people, the Africans, had already started to suffer the calamity of being a defeated and colonised nation.

The struggle for the land, which had lasted for three centuries was over. The whites had won and the Africans were dispossessed of their land. The issue of land ownership and its use became the white man's concern only. Land tenure in white eyes was a matter of monetary transaction and therefore it became a necessity for Africans to buy land or be regarded as squatters.

In contrast to the African tradition of land being allotted to families by the village headman according to family and community needs, the European brought his tradition of land changing hands by means of money. European ideas of money had no place in traditional African economy. Africans were therefore placed in a hopeless position when faced with a foreign concept of land transaction. They had no money.

They were forced off the land by other economic and political measures such as the Land Act of 1913 which displaced thousands of Africans from "white-owned" land, and by the industrial development that followed the discovery of diamonds and gold. African labour was needed in the mines and factories.

By the beginning of the 1900's the mass settlement of Africans in urban areas precipitated a major problem for the mining magnates and the respective governments. The issue was on how the conditions under which Africans occupied land could be changed to meet labour requirements.

There emerged three types of land occupation and housing by and for the Africans. First there was the mass settlement of squatters, secondly a tiny percentage of Africans had acquired freehold property, thirdly there was the introduction of "locations" built by local authorities.

The birth of the labour locations can be traced to the 1903-5 Native Affairs Commission. It proposed "the encouragement of a movement in the direction of individual land-holdings and where practicable the formation of labour locations, in which the Native could reside with his family near his employment. This would largely tend to diminish the number of those intermittent workers in whom absence from their families induces a spirit of restlessness and disinclination to remain in continuous employment". In fact one of the first such urban locations built in 1903, 20 miles south west of Johannesburg City, was Pimville location.

11

Despite the recommendation by the Native Affairs Commission, a new type of housing for Africans developed on the mines. The mining combines decided not to provide married quarters for the entire African labour force. And miners were the majority of African workers. Only a tiny percentage of Africans were thus housed in locations—those employed as interpreters, clerks and teachers, those singled out, by the employers, as an elite group.

Instead barracks or compounds were built for the majority of the African miners. In these barracks the miners lived without their families. It is said that the compounds were not built to meet the desperate housing need, but to combat illicit mineral dealings by African miners and local white traders, as it was estimated that the miners lost between half and one million pounds annually through illicit sales by Africans to dealers. Compound shops were also provided for African miners to buy food and clothing thus further restricting their movement to the mining premises only. Needless to say that profits made in the shops were appropriated to the mining combines. Compounds gave greater control over the labour force.

It was this form of compound housing that the migrant labour system developed with large concentration of workers, and which gave birth to the current migrant labour system of African workers who while on contract are housed in the single-sex urban hostels.

Thus only a fraction of Africans acquired freehold property in places like Alexandra Township and Sophiatown, the two famous Black suburbs which became the main targets of white opposition.

The Shantytowns

Various types of instant settlement were set up by the African men and women who had come to the City to meet the labour demand. One of these shelters, which the labourers put up by mixing clay with sand and using waste material and corrugated iron and asbestos, was called the "shantytown".

This settlement of thirty thousand people ran along a river bank and by a railway line which had a platform called "Orlando Station", eleven miles out from the Johannesburg City. On this convenient site men and women squatted with their families.

The residents of the Shantytown did not buy the plots they built on, nor did they pay land dues to the local authorities. They used the river for water supply and the adjacent bare veld for sanitation. These wall-to-wall, bare, rickety sheds were narrow and dingy, occupying a space of twelve feet by ten. For reference the shacks were divided into groups of Number 1; Number 2; Number 3 and Number 4 areas.

Shantytownians rode on bicycles, some commuted by train to and from the

City where they worked. They were employed in the clothing, furniture, engineering and metallurgical factories as machinists, carpenters, cleaners and messengers. Educated men got jobs as clerks and messengers in the City offices. Some got unskilled jobs like digging tunnels and roads in the construction industries, digging and laying building foundations. Others got jobs as garbage-collectors, gardeners, cooks, nannies and washerwomen in the Johannesburg white suburbs.

People of various African tribes in South Africa, even men from as far as Nyasaland and Rhodesia, Basutoland, Bechuanaland and from Swaziland, merged into a united single African community in the Shantytown.

Here the African Separatist church movement had a large following. Its ministers preached the "gospel" of liberation from bondage. They based their message on the Biblical Old Testament text of Moses leading the children of Israel away from Egyptian captivity. Ironically the Afrikaners' strongest influence was a similar adherence to the Old Testament Bible which made them regard themselves as a second chosen people called by God to a promised land—a second Israel.

In the latter years Shantytownians had their own law courts known as the "Sofasonke Courts" named after Sofasonke Mpanza the man who led them into setting up the squatter settlements. In these courts the inhabitants litigated against each other, parents also brought delinquent youths for punishment. The community had its own unlicensed shops, dairies, butcheries, timber and coal-yards. The shantytown proved to be a thriving market for stolen goods, illicit liquor-brewing and clandestine diamond and gold dealings, as Africans were prohibited by law to buy and drink liquor or to trade in diamonds and gold.

By their action of occupying, without permission, council land, by the forma-tion of the separatist church and by merging into a single African community devoid of tribal conflicts it was clear that the slum dwellers regarded themselves as a community of the dispossessed, oppressed and exploited. This community planted the seeds of the prevailing African national consciousness in urban areas.

As the years went by the Shantytown grew and reached alarming squalor conditions. Later it extended to another group of shelters called "Emasakeni" meaning at the "hessian sheds". Emasakeni was erected about five miles from the Shantytown and fifteen miles from the City.

Sophiatown

As the instant settlements of African squatters were spawning, a black upper-middle-class suburb had emerged, four miles within the confines of the City of Johannesburg.

In this area moneyed Blacks composed of Africans, Indians, Chinese, Coloureds, Japanese, Malayans and Pakistanis built a famous beautiful township known as Sophiatown. Sophiatown, composed of 18,000 plots, was unique in that its residents were of different racial groups and that as a Black community it was located within an exclusive white neighbourhood.

Fate had led Africans to buy plots in Sophiatown. At the time Sophiatown was a sparsely developed area owned by a Mr. Tobiansky who in the last decade of the 19th century had bought land when Johannesburg was still a small mining town planned for future development. He then built houses for sale to whites. But it was at this time that misfortune struck Mr. Tobiansky's ambitious scheme, when the Johannesburg City Council decided to construct a huge sewage disposal system and a location, the Western Native Township, to house three thousand African workers and their families. As soon as this was built whites were no longer prepared to buy his plots and houses. The only thing Mr. Tobiansky could do was to sell his land to Blacks. Thus a Black suburb was created within an exclusively White neighbourhood whose suburbs were spreading in the adjacent areas.

Sophiatown became an embryo of the budding black bourgeoisie. The first overseas-trained African medical practitioner Dr. A. B. Xuma who was also a founder member of the African National Congress was one of the distinguished residents of Sophiatown. Mr. Yusuf Cachalia, a successful businessman and leader of the Transvaal Indian Congress, was also a well-known Sophiatown residence owner and Mr. S. Mabuza, an African businessman, built a thirty thousand rand double storey house in the area. Homeowners consisted of teachers, nurses, businessmen, doctors, traders. Sophiatown was the only urban residential area where Blacks were in keeping with the traditions of White society in that the residents bought land and built smart houses of their own choice. Some of the houses of the landlords "abomasitende" were even equipped with domestic quarters for servants.

Gardens in this suburb were pleasant and attractively cultivated. Its open clean streets had names. Blacks who owned cash used to run their businesses licensed according to proper trading regulations. The businessmen and some homeowners employed workers. Shebeen queens had labourers referred to as "izimbamgodi" meaning "the holediggers" by the Shantytownians. They were called "holediggers" because they dug holes where the shebeen queens hid liquor because Africans were in those days prohibited from drinking and selling liquor. They kept the liquor in drums hidden in underground holes.

In the area there were buildings of the established churches like the Catholic, the famous Christ the King Anglican and the Lutheran churches. Nearby there was the Coronation Hospital and Bridgeman Memorial Hospital—the latter for maternity cases. The children attended schools situated in the centre of the town like St. Peter's Anglican School, a famous Eton of South Africa. This school was also integrated. The Young Women's Christian Association, a worldwide organisation, had a branch here whose president and founder member was Mrs. Madie-Hall Xuma, the Afro-American wife of Dr. Xuma.

In short residents here regarded themselves as an integral part of the developing middle-class society. They were careful to make a distinction between living in the suburbia of Sophiatown and being an inhabitant of a location like Western Native Township, Pimville or Orlando. To a Sophiatown family it was a symbol of permanency, racial equality and elegance to live in a property-owned suburb unlike living with the squatters of the Shantytown or the Council-owned labour depots—the locations.

My Grandfather

One such aspiring resident was my grandfather. He moved to Johannesburg from the Mapumulo district of Natal when he was a teenage boy. And judging by the account of his childhood life, his educational process and the date of the birth of his first child, he must have been born not later than 1890.

He was born of a polygamous family—his father had three wives, my grandfather's mother being the youngest and third; my grandfather was her only child but he was the eldest son in the whole family "kraal" unit. It is significant that his father named him "Mbulawa", meaning "the possible one to be harmed". This name was symbolic in that it was the first wife of a kraal who by tradition was expected to give birth to an heir. Because Mbulawa was born of the third wife, his father presumed that in case one of the first two wives gave birth to a son, subsequently she might be envious and harm Mbulawa for the benefit of her own son. Later sons were born of my great-grandfather's two wives and Mbulawa was not harmed.

What moved Mbulawa from the kraal was that his mother was interested in getting him educated. By this time in the district there was a Lutheran Mission Station where Africans were being converted to Christianity. So Mbulawa was encouraged by his mother to attend the catechism lessons. He started the lessons at the age when he was already herding and milking cows. In those days he could have been 10 to 14 years old. Because of the ease in which he mastered the catechism, he was baptised. He chose his own Christian name "Absolum". The minister in charge of the Mission was so impressed by his intelligence that he offered to train Absolum as a cook and asked him to attend night school. When my grandfather discussed the offer with his mother, she agreed. Absolum had, therefore, to leave the family unit and move to the Mission Station. Having received his mother's approval, he departed with ease. There were no suitcases to pack.

A tragic misfortune, which my grandfather always mentioned as having made his mother determined to see him leave the kraal, had happened early one evening as he was herding the cattle back to their shed. A thunderstorm was gathering momentum, when suddenly a thunderbolt struck at the family huts. "I became blind momentarily", he would describe, "when from the huts a ball of fire shot to the sky". The cattle bellowed as they ran amuck in panic. As for him, he regained consciousness lying askew on the long grass. He jumped up and ran home as fast as his legs could carry him, to find his mother's hut burnt to the ground. The wailing mothers were running around with their arms in the air in search of the children who had been inside the huts. The rasping sounds of panic-stricken dogs, cats and fowls added a funeral note to the confusion. Later after a search, the charred body of one of his brothers was found lying a distance from the kraal. By chance, his mother was not in the hut when the thunderbolt struck.

Speaking in confidence to him, his mother was convinced that the thunderbolt had claimed the wrong boy; it had been meant for her son Mbulawa. Soon after the tragedy, the minister responsible for the Mission Station was transferred to Johannesburg and took "Absolum" along. "But before I left", my grandfather was certain to tell us, "my mother had become a Christian. I chose her name and saw her baptised", he would proudly add. I have often wondered if great-grandmother deserted the polygamous family unit after having become a Christian.

By the time my grandfather arrived in Johannesburg, he was a seasoned cook on pay by the parish. He continued with night school and took a theology course. A few years later he was ordained as Reverend Absolum M. Sikakane. He became one of the first African ministers of the urban Lutheran Church. Immediately after ordination he set out to look for a wife. He was determined to marry an urban woman who could cook European-style meals and, in his own words, "prepare a salad". He wanted a wife who could read and write, dressed neatly and knew how to look after the home of a minister. He did not have to look far. At the home of an African landlord in 1st Avenue, Alexandra Township, he met and married Miss Bellinah Mbanjwa (who had been born and brought up in this urban area).

The Lutheran Church allocated the Rev. Sikakane a parish right in the heart of Johannesburg, in an area called Doornfontein. The main purpose of this parish was to cater for the spiritual needs of the growing black urban population living in the heart of the white city and its residential areas. The congregation were domestic workers and their families, the inmates of the office cleaners' quarters, and home-owners from the black suburbs of Sophiatown and Alexandra. His congregation was occasionally sprinkled with "liberal" European Christians.

In February 1916 my father was born in Alexandra Township, at my grandmother's home. In those days it was the usual practice that a woman gave birth to her first baby while under the care of her own parents. My father was christened Jonathan Mandlenkosi Sikakane.

While living in the parish, my grandfather bought two plots of land in Alexandra Township. He was preparing to build a house where he could retire. As the political situation moved to a truly racially segregated society, my grandfather's plans failed to materialise.

16

Five more children were born to the family. One died in his youth, and in the middle of the 1930's my grandmother died too. Both are buried at Croesus Cemetery, where at that time Africans could buy burial ground. Today Africans are not allowed to bury their dead there.

In Johannesburg my grandfather did not only look after the spiritual needs of the black workers, he became active in the political activities of the African National Congress, which at the time was involved in the campaign for the basic political right of the African people to participate in the country's government machinery. In his pulpit he denounced the "satanic voice of the white racists who were hell-bent to exclude, for-ever-amen, the black people from taking part in the government of the country". As a Christian he stood for a united non-racial society.

On the effects of continuous racial discrimination suffered by the black community he had a lot to castigate the white-controlled church about. The domestics lived in one-roomed quarters, with attached cubicles as shower-rooms, some of which had open-holed toilets on the floor. Their beds were mounted four feet high close to the wall. At night a sheet was used as a curtain to provide privacy against the children sleeping on the floor. Once the children reached school-going age, they had to part from their parents to stay with relatives or friends in areas with schools. In the "locations-in-the-sky" African men had to smuggle in their wives at night because it was illegal for unauthorised persons to be found on such premises. These locations-in-the-sky were, in fact, storerooms of high-rise city buildings. In these rooms the office-cleaners would find shelter to sleep after working hours.

The Rev. Sikakane called for proper health facilities because endemic disease was rife and infantile mortality highest in the squatter areas. No Christian should turn a blind eye to such waste of life. He promised that hell-fire was waiting for the perpetrators of such crime. He attributed to racial hatred and greed the plans to move African landowners from property bought with money they had earned by "sweating blood".

He complained that young people "in these days" were no longer having "white weddings" in church. There had developed a system, dubbed "vat en sit", meaning practically "let's marry on our own without conforming to family tradition and the church." This deplorable practice was happening because men could not afford to foot the wedding bill, let alone to pay a "dowry." It was the low wages which were contributing to the development of a "permissive society." As the Rev. Sikakane moved around spreading the gospel among the workers, he was more and more appalled by their living and working conditions.

On a number of occasions he was taken to task by the white-dominated Lutheran synod for indulging in politics instead of comforting the souls of the oppressed. After all was he not a pagan pastoral herdboy when he was discovered and civilised! He did not give in.

A few years after the death of his wife, my grandfather got married to a school-teacher to conform with the Church standards, which did not approve of a wifeless spiritual leader. This marriage soon went on the rocks. He did not hesitate to start divorce proceedings against his wife. The Church synod objected, arguing that he was setting a bad example. The Rev. Sikakane was an unyielding person once he had embarked on a course of action. He divorced the woman, and was immediately ordered to retire by the church.

By this time, the Nationalist government was in power, and the writing was on the wall for African property owners. My grandfather sold his land in Alexandra Township and bought land in Clermont Township, Durban, an area which was many miles distant from the white city, and had not featured as a "blackspot" threatened with removal, like Sophiatown and Alexandra Township.

He thus returned to Natal, but did not even dream of returning to his village of Mapumulo because he regarded himself as a detribalised African. He believed that by buying land and property he was building a secure future for his children. In those days Mapumulo was designated as a "reserve"; it was not yet determined in terms of the gigantic "Bantustan" development and its future was still undecided.

On arrival in Clermont Township, my grandfather rented a four-roomed house, while making plans to build his own house. The plans took years to materialise because it is almost impossible for Africans to raise mortgages in that country. From the scant information I gathered as the adult members of the family were discussing the issue, he took a housing contract with a firm which undertook to build standardised housing for African landowners. I do not know what the conditions of contract were, but the size and shape of those houses which sprang up all over Clermont were similar to the drab four-roomed houses in Soweto.

The developments which drove my grandfather to move to Clermont were part of the continuous attempt by white authorities local and central to control and curb African residence in urban areas. There were many reasons for their doing this.

The Southwest Locations

The slums were a breeding ground of fatal contagious diseases. With no sanitation, smallpox and tuberculous diseases took their toll. Such outbreaks alarmed the white governments who feared the spread of deadly diseases to the white community.

By the 1930's local authorities and government were also alarmed at the rapid expansion of the squatter areas. They feared they would lose more and more land to uncontrolled African communities.

In a bid to end and control such settlements as the Shantytown, the Johannesburg City Council built more and more houses to the South West outskirts of the City for African settlement. This happened from the late 1930's onwards.

Here along the line of rail more urban African residential locations were built. These tiny two to three roomed enclaves formed three locations named after the three railway stations near each site. They were Mlamlamkunzi, Orlando and Pimville. The construction of these three locations heralded the birth of the largest modern ghetto in Africa where over a million African workers live today.

The creation of these locations was only one example of the general development of other large African locations in many South African cities in the years following the mining and industrial revolution.

More and more Africans were arriving in Johannesburg to work—and more and more were needed by growing industries and services. This was necessary and at the same time seen as a danger. As the urban African population increased, this rise spelt out the revolutionary possibilities presented by the urban African masses who could be mobilized against a social order that denied them equality.

The numbers and permanency of Africans in the urban areas thus became the central issue to white politicians who, as the 1922 Stallard Commission recorded, wanted that "Natives must only enter the urban areas to minister to the needs of the white man." (Quoted in the *Oxford History of South Africa* p. 191).

Following the growth of towns, repeated accusations were made that many of the Africans in the towns were "surplus" or "idle" undesirables who were responsible for much of the violent crime that occurred in the towns. But in fact the great majority of the male shack-dwellers were usefully employed in the city. Similar findings were reported of the African squatters who crowded around Johannesburg, where at one time the Council was even prepared to let the Government take all the squatters away. The result of the subsequent enumerations showed that had this been done, the effect on the economic life of Johannesburg would have been like that of a major strike. The squatters stayed, and ultimately had to be given more adequate housing. They had demonstrated that they were not "temporary sojourners."

In 1939 in a desperate attempt to limit land occupation by squatters, emergency camps were established by municipalities in urban areas. The Johannesburg municipalities, for instance, built the Moroka camps which accommodated 60,000 people.

Many Africans also lived in the backyards of the white residential areas, and many others at the top apartments of the skyscrapers mushrooming in town. This gave rise to the jocular name of "locations in the sky". Africans living in the backyards of the white residential areas were said to be staying at "emakhishini" meaning at the "kitchens."

When the Afrikaner Nationalist Party came to power in 1948 with its policy of apartheid it was denied that a permanently urbanized African population existed. "All the Bantu have their permanent homes in the reserves and their entry into other areas and into the urban centres is merely of a temporary nature and for economic reasons" was their policy.

The apartheid regime was determined to "reverse the flow" of blacks from the towns, while at the same time being deeply committed to industrial expansion and economic growth. So as soon as it took office, the regime was determined to implement the policy of apartheid to its logical conclusion.

In pursuance of its policy in the urban areas of Johannesburg the first Herculean task was the removal of Sophiatown and Alexandra suburbs where Africans owned freehold properties. The Shantytown had to be demolished and as soon as it was feasible the entire African labour population housed in the south west locations had to be converted into a migrant labour force.

The disposition of the south west areas was ideal for the grand apartheid strategy of rehousing the African people. The area was not only of an adequate distance from the white town, it had already a number of locations housing a registered labour force. There was also a rail link to commute African workers to and from the city. Huge industrial areas separated the locations from the city and exclusive white suburbs. No expanding white residential areas could encircle it and buffer areas existed to ensure complete detachment of African residential areas from the city where they worked. On expansion the south west locations could connect with other African townships within the Witwatersrand.

The foundations had been laid and the apartheid government quickly moved in with more bricks and mortar.

Demolition and Eviction

The rickety shacks which composed the Shantytowns were built on land which fell under the jurisdiction of the Johannesburg City Council on which the apartheid regime exerted pressure to have this white man's land cleared of the squatters. The mass removals and resettlement started in the 1950's.

The bulldozing to the ground of the shelters was done with ease by officialdom. The inhabitants had welcomed it as they had been living under conditions of extreme squalor. But the rehousing of the people from the Shantytowns also meant the screening of persons by local authorities. People had to be granted official permission in order to reside in the new locations—in short, the location tenants had to be registered and employed. By the time this mass removal and resettlement was in momentum thousands of "illegal Africans" became victims of the screening process.

First it was Africans from outside the South African borders who had come to seek work in the city of gold. They were men, and many of them married South African women. Those expatriate African men employed in the mines were sent to live in the mine compounds and forbidden entry into the locations. Those who were employed in the city were repatriated to their countries of origin. Thousands of such African men were affected and it was a sorrowful time for their wives who had to depart with their husbands, leaving relatives behind. Some men left without their wives and children because when discovered they were immediately detained in police cells and repatriated if it was found that they came from outside the South African borders.

Those single African men who came from within South Africa but from outside the city and whose origin could be traced to the "reserves" and could not prove that they had been in urban areas for more than ten years, were housed in the single-sex hostels provided they were employed. Those who were deemed "idle" were endorsed out of the urban areas and sent to the reserves.

Sophiatown, where Africans owned freehold rights, had to go because in the eyes of the apartheid regime such rights for Africans symbolized a permanency that was incompatible with the concept of urban Africans being temporary sojourners. Black spots in white areas had to be done away with.

The legislation to remove African home-owners from Sophiatown met with strong resistance. It was a bitter blow to the African residents who lost freehold rights and the freedom to live in communities not subjected to the rigorous controls encountered in ordinary municipal townships. Slums undoubtedly did exist, but there were also substantial houses. An African leader remarked "We deny that this is a slum clearance scheme, because to eliminate slum conditions you do not have to shift a whole community, nearly 60,000 people, you do not have to condemn the good with the bad, you do not have to divest people of their property rights."

The resistance put up by the African home owners supported by the African National Congress was so strong that the government had to call in troops with armoured trucks, dogs and bulldozers to remove and carry the residents to the new townships. The pattern of re-housing the residents was similar to the re-settlement of the people from the shantytowns. But with the establishment of the Resettlement Board apartheid demands were met in housing people according to ethnic groupings

The greatest victory of the apartheid regime in having removed the "black spot"—Sophiatown—was that immediately on those ruins an exclusive white modern suburb was built; it was named Triomf, an Afrikaans word for triumph. It was indeed brute triumph for the apartheid regime in its determined efforts to keep urban areas white.

The new doctrine of apartheid aimed at ruthless segregation and the keeping of Africans in a state of primitive dependency for ever. It was a determined attempt to turn the clock back, for modern developments had inevitably brought changes to South Africa. My own family history illustrated this.

My Father and Mother

My father is what I could describe as a typical schooled "Joburgher" at heart. From infancy his world was that of a cosmopolitan nature. In the city there were Church-run day schools, which in principle were open to children of all racial groups, but were predominantly filled by black pupils. On odd occasions a European pupil would be enrolled. Jonathan Sikakane was a pupil of one such school. In the city streets he played hide-and-seek in the backyards of Indian, Chinese, Coloured or white premises. Children of this community enjoyed attending the various national festivals, like the Chinese Dragon celebration, the Indian Divali and Christmas.

He was enrolled for secondary education at a boarding school in Roodepoort, run by the Lutheran Church. Years later, when the Nationalists took power, this school was immediately shut down because it was located in an Afrikaans stronghold. It had always been a thorn in the flesh of the Nationalists. My father obtained distinctions in English and Zulu in his matriculation examination.

In 1940 he married a schoolteacher he had met at a tennis tournament. My mother had travelled with a team from Newcastle, Natal, to Johannesburg to compete in a tennis tournament. After the marriage, they lived for a while in Doornfontein.

My mother's maiden name was Amelia Nxumalo. She was born in Newcastle, her father being of mixed race (his mother European and father Swazi). Her mother came from Swaziland where she was related to the royal family. My mother spoke of Prince Makhosini, the present prime minister of Swaziland, as having lived with her family while attending school in Newcastle. The Nxumalo family to which my mother belonged is known to have direct connections with the Swazi royalty.

The Newcastle area where my mother grew up was predominantly composed of people of mixed race. It was also declared a "white spot" by the apartheid regime, and the people were removed into other locations. Its population was split into African and Coloured. For many of the inhabitants the official race classification depended on how straight or kinky the hair was, or how dark or fair the skin was. Those whose fair complexion and straight hair made them look "white", but suspected otherwise by the race classification board, had blood tests taken and were examined for mongolian blue spots. My mother's family was split into Coloured and Africans. Those fairer members of the family, who were classified Coloured, now live in Johannesburg, in Kliptown, a Coloured area bordering Soweto.

My parents' moved to Orlando location, which is now part of Soweto. The registered Native male house tenant J. M. Sikakane, moved into No. 7703 Orlando West, in 1940. Listed in his house permit, as dependants, were the names of his wife, daughter, two brothers and sisters. Reflected on the house permit were the places where each person was born and on what date. Also enclosed in the house file is the copy of the male's marriage certificate. This precious file is kept in the Orlando Municipal Office. To the native male Sikakane and his dependants this record meant they were desirable natives of the urban area of Johannesburg.

The Sikakane family moved into a standard four-roomed house, one of the few equipped with a shower-room. The lavatory was outside. A monthly rent was paid to the municipal office.

Three years later, I was born at the Bridgeman Memorial Maternity Hospital. This was a private hospital run by a missionary society. Its privacy was not in a lavish sense of a mother having her own room and special treatment—it was in the sense that a patient had to pay to be sure of a safe birth at the standard of the National Health service hospitals in Britain. Otherwise women had to deliver in their unhygienic crowded homes.

The Bridgeman Maternity Hospital was situated in a white residential area. So when the apartheid regime took power this hospital had to be closed because black babies could not be born in a white area. I suppose the very first cries of newly-born black babies disturbed the peace of the white residential areas. Like all institutions which served blacks in white areas, this maternity home was shut down by the apartheid regime.

My parents named me Joyce, and my grandfather added the Zulu name Nomafa, which means "inheritance". When flattering myself, I am inclined to believe that he named me thus, so that I should continue with the political struggle he was involved in with the African National Congress, fighting against white domination. He had named my elder sister Themb'umusa, which meant "have faith in mercy." By the time I was born, it had become obvious that the African people could have no faith in any mercy, the political struggle had to be pursued with full vigour. The family abbreviated my sister's name to Thembie. She failed to pronounce my name correctly, and would instead utter "Fufu." From then on my playmates and everyone in the location called me "Fufu."

The Growth of Soweto

The 1950's saw the phenomenal growth of Soweto. A special law, the Bantu Building Workers Act, was passed, making it possible for African artisans to be trained and employed in constructing the locations.

In building the houses the local authorities designed a "belt system" whereby foundations were laid first for a series of houses, then concrete floors, brick or concrete walls put up, ending with asbestos roofs. The houses are without bathrooms and internal doors. Inmates are left to finish at their own cost the plastering of walls, the erection of ceilings and filling of gaps on brick walls and window panes. It is against the law to put up any extension, such as a bathroom.

The Native Service Levy Act of 1952 was passed to tax employers to contribute to the housing scheme. The employers got their money refunded by paying low wages to African workers. A six million rand loan from the mining industry, initiated by Sir Ernest Oppenheimer, was granted to the Johannesburg Municipality in 1958. This loan enabled local authorities to speed up its segregated housing scheme. No wonder that white overseas tourists who are taken on a bus tour to Soweto have tea and cake in a luxurious tea-room, beautifully appointed with wood furnishings and facing, through scenic plateglass windows, on to the well-kept Ernest Oppenheimer Park. This park and tea-room, in the heart of Soweto, is for whites only. Its function is to provide free tea and coffee to the white tourists, and acts as a venue for white official functions.

It is estimated that between 1952 and 1972 about 400,000 houses were built in Soweto. During this period another kind of housing scheme was allowed to appease the Sophiatown home-owners who were bitterly opposed to the removal scheme. Vacant land was made available where the moneyed Africans could buy plots and build houses on a 90-year leasehold. In the same area the standard four-roomed houses built were also put on the 90-year leasehold market. In this area, named Dube, it is estimated that 2,000 owner-built and council-built houses were bought under this scheme.

No sooner had the government succeeded in resettling the Africans en masse, it reduced the leasehold to 30 years and then in 1967 legislation was passed to abolish even the remaining 30-year leases. This legislation was a direct act of expropriation. Some Duberites tried to grumble, but failed. The community's wishful effort to keep in the same stride as that of their masters was curtailed. Like all other Soweto tenants, the Duberites are now propertyless and are paying stipulated monthly rentals for their houses. Because of the high rents and the shortage of housing, Dube houses are gradually rented to single-room occupants. Thus the one time show-piece of African advancement is being reduced to multi-occupation.

African home ownership is a political issue in South Africa. Whites, of course, are allowed to freely buy and sell houses to live where they choose, and bequeath their property to their spouses and children. Not so Africans in the urban areas. They are always tenants without security. If a man dies, his widow is not allowed to stay. Recently the government has re-introduced 30 year leases as a "concession".

When I was growing up, the separate locations that make up Soweto were all known by their individual names. When asked where one lived, one would answer, "I live in Orlando," or Pimville, or wherever. Today it is just "Soweto."

The new locations of South West Townships were built to accommodate the workers needed by the capital's industries—but they were never sufficient. Almost all Soweto houses are overcrowded. Ours in Orlando township, just north of the areas where all the development was taking place, was no exception.

As it was listed in the permit, in the four-roomed house we lived with my two uncles and my two aunts who were boarding at educational institutions and came home for holidays. By this time my grandfather had moved to Durban. Uncles Solly and Mike were working in the city. Invariably relatives and friends who were without houses also put-up with us. This was done without official knowledge because my parents and uncles were full-time workers who saw no point in joining queues, at the municipal office, seeking visitors' permits when having to shelter other homeless workers.

Pass Laws

Permits are needed for everything. The law states that no-one may lawfully reside in Soweto or other locations without being in possession of several appropriate permits. To make sure that this law is complied with, the search for "illegal" natives is carried out by the "blackjacks," the notorious municipal police. This police outfit is nicknamed "blackjacks" because its members are dressed in black from head to toe. At night their complexion blends with that of the uniform. Walking in the streets at dusk, you can only figure them out by the click-crunch sound of their heavy black boots. The jackets of their uniforms are double-breasted, fastened with shiny copper-coloured buttons. On their heads are black caps, the brims cover the forehead leaving room for the ferocious looking eyes, as if they were the eyes of blood-thirsty hunting hounds. The hunt for the "illegal" natives is done at anytime of the day, but the "blackjacks" seem to enjoy the night chase and that of the snug hours of two to five a.m.

During the night raids, the "blackjacks" would bang on the door with "knob-kerries", flashing torches on the windows. They would yell "open the door, it's the police." The whole neighbourhood was awoken. A delay in opening meant the maddening jackboot kicks on the door, which invariably was followed by the blackjack stampede into the house as the door fell on the floor (there were always disputes between the tenants and the municipality on who was re-sponsible for the door repair bills). In the rush, they would flash torches on the inmates' faces as they snatched the blankets, counting the number of heads under the blankets. Men were usually caught in their underpants, women in their birthday suits would scramble for a portion of blanket or sheet to keep their privacy covered, as the blackjackets pulled away the blankets for a count.

In the prevailing darkness, one of the inmates will stumble around the room in search of a matchbox to light a candle and find the "dompasses" to prove to the policemen that they are registered workers. But proof of being a registered worker is not sufficient for the municipal police whose concern is the "house permit" only.

Their captives are not given time to dress. Jumping into a coat is the only salvation. To illustrate the drama of these raids, there is a popular story of a man who ran out naked through the back-door of a house as the blackjacks got through the front door. Unfortunately for him, he was later apprehended hiding in the loo. Without asking any questions, the blackjacks marched him, in his birthday suit, to the municipal office. On the following morning they delivered him, naked as he was, before the superintendent, alleging that they had caught a "witch" in someone's yard. Later in the day the man's brother went to the office and identified him as his "dependant" who had gone for a pee just as the blackjacks arrived for the raid. The superintendent warned him of the law's requirements, and that next time he would lose the tenancy of the house if he did not comply with the law. It is needless to add that the standard bribe for each victim caught was ten shillings for the blackjacks and more for the belligerent superintendent.

We children were terrified by these raids. We clung on to the slippery torsos of our parents screaming our lungs out with terror.

As if the jackboot terror of the blackjacks is not enough on the lives of Sowetonians, as soon as they set foot on the streets, they are pounced upon by units of the South African Police, whose prime interest is the "dompass" and the search for "dangerous weapons". By law, an African is not allowed to carry a stick, even a walking stick. The Sowetonians call the SAP's "amakgathas" meaning "the arseholes."

When pouncing on his victim the policeman will say "Hy'ta, pass jong"—meaning "Hey, pass, man". Without a murmer the African quickly produces the "stinker." Failure to produce immediately on demand means instant arrest with a charge of "obstructing the police while performing his duty". Having taken out the pass from your pocket, the policeman snatches it from your hand. He takes his time paging through it. First he looks at the polaroid photograph and then looks at your face menacingly to make certain it is your profile on the pass, he then reads the domicile stamp, the labour registration stamp and the month-end signature of your employer. The domicile stamp certifies that you are allowed by law to reside in the particular location, the labour registration stamp complements the first in that you are allowed to reside in the urban area whilst employed, and the month-end signature of your employer in fact testifies that you are in regular employment. Failure to produce the pass or to meet any of the above requirements means on-the-spot arrest. Then follows the hands-up order. The policeman conducts a quick body frisk, and empties your pockets in search of "dangerous weapons."

This "hunt" for "illegal or vagrant Bantus" can be repeated several times on one person in one trip from Soweto to work in the city. A worker can have it done in his street, the next street, at the bus terminus or railway station, inside the bus or train, at the point of arrival and at any street leading to the place of work.

In the streets the workers arrested on pass offences are handcuffed in two's and marched in silence in a column from street to street until the officers on duty finish their shift. Then all the apprehended workers are taken to a police station. It can take three or more days before victims are processed and appear in court. The relatives are not notified of the arrest. It has become an accepted practice that should a person over 16 years of age be missing from home, the search is first for his "dompass" lest he left it in the house. If by luck a person gets arrested and is seen by someone else who knows him and his family, then the family gets to hear and knows where to go and look. It is illegal to ask a policeman or the person arrested the reason for an arrest. "Inquisitive" persons get arrested and charged with obstructing the police in the execution of their duty.

As children we used to enjoy the illegal game of warning adults whenever we sighted "amaphoyisa"—the police—hiding in corners waiting for their prey.

The early 1950's were also the days of "liquor prohibition," thus the liquor squad raids were at their peak. As we were playing games in the dusty streets we children could sense the "kwela-kwela" vans as they came roaring fast from a distance. Our high-pitched voices singing "ikwela-kwela" would reverberate through each location. Responding to the alarm call those men and women inside the matchbox houses who were either brewing or drinking liquor would either hide it, spill it or drink it up and run out, or stagger out, of the houses to escape arrest. It was fun for us to see the police run a wild goose chase. Should some people get caught in an area we would hear voices of wailing children as women and men were escorted into the "kwela-kwela" vans with all the confiscated booze. Some women would be carrying babies on their backs. Today, despite the lifting of liquor prohibition, the police liquor raids are as alive as ever before because of the "shebeens." Shebeens are the homes where the Sowetonians can go and buy liquor "on tick" and drink "after hours," rather than in the official municipal beerhalls.

Another police unit which brings terror down the spines of Soweto residents is that of the "Murder and Robbery Squad" which raids homes on the slightest suspicion and rumour. Members of this squad are armed and do not hesitate to fire. Sowetonians call officers of the Murder and Robbery Squad "skiet en donker," meaning "those who shoot in the dark" because this unit seems to enjoy shooting people at night. Many a time Sowetonians—the youth in particular—have been shot and killed by "flying" bullets of this unit. The newspapers report such killings as "thugs killed in gun battle with police." In a country where it is illegal for an African to carry a stick one wonders where on earth can an African youth lay his hand on a gun.

At the same time the crime rate in Soweto is high, and the police do little to curb it. Black lives and property do not receive the same protection as white.

Crime

By increasing insecurity, destroying families and depriving Africans of all rights and hope, apartheid has obviously created a class of dehumanised beings in Soweto. These notorious thugs are called "tsotsis." This fearless, declassed element indiscriminately robs, assaults, rapes and kills other Soweto dwellers.

Soweto, South Africa's most densely populated black urban area, is said to have the world's highest murder rate. More than 420 murder cases were reported in Soweto during the first half of 1974. And from July 1, 1974, to June 1975 the figure reached 701 murders.

There are 6 police stations in Soweto, manned by 1,306 uniformed police and 681 reservists, for a total population of over one million.

"The American city of Boston is reported to have 500 murders a year," said

Colonel J. P. Visser of the Soweto Murder Squad to a reporter of the *Sunday Tribune*. "And it has been claimed Boston has the highest murder rate in the world. But here in Soweto we handle nearly twice that amount each year," Colonel Visser is reported to have boasted. He disclosed that of the 420 murders investigated, 76 per cent led to prosecution and only 2 per cent of those resulted in murder convictions. The balance of prosecutions resulted in convictions of culpable homicide and lesser categories because a prime mitigation factor in most cases was that the killers were usually under the influence of alcohol and that the killings usually occurred spontaneously and were therefore unpremeditated. (*Sunday Tribune* 24/11/74).

From what Colonel Visser says it is clear that Mr. Average Soweto Sojourner is not born a murderer, he is moulded by the repressive and exploitative system into a drunken and stupefied killer.

To illustrate how the social conditions and the indifference of the police force shocked a judge here is an example reported in the *Rand Daily Mail* of 27/9/75:

NOTES FROM A HEADMASTER'S LOGBOOK...

In the Rand Supreme Court this week Mr. Justice Botha found nine Africans guilty of a killing. Yet he suspended passing of sentence for three years because he was so appalled by the conditions under which the accused—two teachers and seven pupils—lived in Phiri Township in Soweto.

"I cannot shut my eyes to the fact that people in that area live under the terror of thugs," the judge said. "I cannot tell you how upset I am by these conditions."

After convicting the nine Africans of culpable homicide—they had killed an alleged member of the notorious ZX5 gang—and of five counts of assault with intent to do grievous bodily harm and one of malicious damage to property, the judge listened to evidence in mitigation from the headmaster of the schoolchildren involved, Mr. S. Sechefo of Phiri Higher Primary School.

Each day during the morning breaks, the thugs would mix with his pupils in the nearby shops. They would force money from the boys or drag some of the girls to their neighbourhood hide-outs.

At the end of the break, Mr. Sechefo would find he was minus one or two girl students. Some of these girls would return to classes at noon, weeping and ashamed to tell him of what had happened to them. The other girls would be away for longer periods, and he would report the incidents to Moroka police station.

Mr. Sechefo said it seemed the thugs kept a timetable of the school's activities. They would be at functions in the local halls, the sports fields and also mix with pupils when the school visited the zoo.

Sometimes Mr. Sechefo had to drive wounded students to Baragwanath Hospital and pay for their treatment. Many times he drove to Moroka police station to report such incidents.

When the police made no attempt to investigate the activities of the gang, he decided to enter the daily events in a "log book." These are some of the entries:

19/6/73: On arrival at school today, I found the fence around the yard had been cut and the iron poles dug out. I reported the matter to the police, and gave them the names of the suspects. The police did nothing about the matter and I gave it up.

16/2/74: On arrival at school today I found that the thugs had smashed the windows of the school cottage and damaged the caretaker's car. Matter reported to the police, and when they did nothing about it, the school did the repairs.

22/2/74: On arrival at school today I found that my office and the storeroom had been burgled. A number of school items estimated at the value of R339 were stolen. Matter reported to the police who did nothing about it. But as a result of information I received from one of my pupils, I requested the police to accompany me to a certain house in the neighbourhood where I found the stolen goods. A middle-aged man was arrested and later convicted.

31/10/74: Today on arrival at school from the examination centre, I received a report that thugs had stopped some of my pupils from coming to school. This was followed by a fight that resulted in the death of one of the thugs and the wounding of five thugs.

Brigadier W. F. J. Meyer, Divisional Commissioner of the police in Soweto, said this week that the young thugs in the street and shop corners were the responsibility of their parents. Police could not bundle and lock them up for loitering in the streets, he said.

Commenting on Soweto's crime, Mr. Lennox Mlonzi, a member of the Urban Bantu Council, described it as "a by-product of the capitalist and racist laws of the South African government." (*Rand Daily Mail* 25/11/74).

Addressing the Johannesburg Black Committee of the National Institute of Crime Prevention and Rehabilitation of Offenders, Mr. Mlonzi demanded that Pretoria (government's citadel) should answer for it—Mr. Mlonzi's son had been murdered in Soweto the previous year. He asked how crime could be minimised in an apartheid society. If it could not be completely eradicated then the crime rate must be brought down as much as possible, but this cannot be done without shaking the very fundamental principle of the present government—apartheid.

When it suits them, the police give blessing to the formation of tribal vigilante groups and courts known as "makgotla." By law such formations are illegal, but because these tribal vigilante patrols and courts deal with crime on sectional bases, not as a community and national issue, the police tolerate them. One such "makgotla" is run by a woman, Sinah Makume, also named Madipere which means Mother of the Horses. This woman's money-making business is that of collecting empty liquor bottles and selling them back to the municipal bottle stores. She is a former policewoman escort, a job which meant escorting victims of influx control laws to the Bantustan wasteland. Madipere's role is clearly that of a state agent.

Following the 1976 demonstrations and shootings in Soweto, it was reported in the *Scotsman* 6/9/76 that:

"The Justice Minister, Mr. James Kruger, is considering giving legal status to tribal vigilante groups in the townships, according to reliable sources today.

These groups, known as makgotla, have operated unofficially in Soweto for several years. They work by tribal law and occasionally administer public floggings.

A group of makgotla leaders met Mr. Kruger last week. The sources said he had told them that he was thinking of giving them legal status through the Urban Bantu Council, elected black bodies who have a mainly advisory role.

The makgotla said they wanted to act independently, with full power to settle family disputes and deal with 'disobedient children.' This could apply to schoolchildren, thousands of whom have boycotted schools and joined in rioting and intimidation during recent weeks."

Sowetonians do not only suffer from location brutality, but also that of the police force. According to a typical terror toll of the South African Police, fifty Africans were shot and killed by police in the first six months of 1974. Policemen also wounded 50 Africans, twenty-seven Coloureds and four whites, and fourteen juveniles (seven Africans, six Coloured and one Asian) throughout the country.

Justice meted out to white and black criminals is not the same. Black men are sentenced to death when convicted of aggravated robbery and rape when the victims are white. Yet whites who kill, rape and grievously assault blacks receive very light suspended sentences. A very recent case is that of Cecilia Maria Liebenberg, a white woman, who shot dead a thirteen-year-old African school-girl while allegedly stealing fruit with a group of friends, and was fined R204. The father of Frieda Moathodi found his daughter's fully-clothed skeleton a month after the incident with evidence of bullet marks. This happened in Johannesburg.

The Economic Aspect

Poverty is the over-riding aspect of economic life in Soweto. First of all it has to be asked if the people of Soweto own any capital, and the answer is NO. Soweto has a white economic infra-structure. Those who wish to refute this cannot identify more than a zero fraction of doctors, lawyers and businessmen in Soweto who own accumulated cash. How they earned it, we shall argue later. Going back to the first point, we can only know of the financial standing of the people of Soweto by looking at the sum total of their average earnings and purchasing power.

A Soweto household of five needed in 1974 a monthly income of R108·66 to survive, according to poverty lines drawn up by academics. And yet the average wages of Sowetonians ranged from R40 to R80 a month. Their earnings are below the barest poverty datum line. By adding the annual total wages and purchasing power of Soweto's million population statisticians arrive at millions and millions of rands as the "wealth" of the area. On paper these millions of rands look like accumulated capital and yet it is money spent on essential bare necessities leaving no cents for savings. Whites take home 72% of the national income and the blacks only 28%, and the situation has remained unchanged for the last fifteen years, according to the 5 April 1974 issue of the *Financial Mail* (South Africa).

Those African workers who have bank accounts are by and large the white collar workers who earn above R80 a month and whose wages are deposited by their employers on their behalf in the bank. They must have bank savings accounts in order to draw their wages from the bank. By denying themselves essential needs like nutritious food or an extra pair of socks or shoes, these workers are able to save a few cents in their accounts. The zero fraction of the professional class which owns capital got it because the system allows uncontrolled medical fees to be paid to doctors, and the lawyers charge exorbitant fees in criminal, divorce and insurance cases—like motor accident cases. One or two members of this class own shares and bonds. What is ludicrous is that, because of apartheid, these investors cannot sit at any shareholders meeting because whites own all the industries of the country and the apartheid laws forbid mixed meetings.

Soweto's businessmen have been successfully squeezed out of real money-making because the government does not allow them more than one trading licence, thus stifling any business growth. It is virtually impossible for Africans to get loans because they do not own land and therefore cannot get mortgages. Thus an African businessman who lives in Dube in an expensive house, and was one-time president of the Johannesburg Chamber of Commerce, was refused an overdraft because he could offer no security. Those who are still surviving are men of independent cash (for instance Richard Maponya has made the bulk of his fortune by betting the winning horses in some of the Rand's July Handicaps, whose sweepstakes are hundreds and thousands of rands) and those acting as branches of the giant supermarkets in the City. Talk is rife in Soweto that some of those businessman who own cash got it through dubious means like collaborating with the "system" against the national struggle, through robbery, illicit liquor, diamond and gold dealings.

The government has decreed that "trading by Bantu in white areas is not an inherent primary opportunity for them." So would-be African entrepreneurs who want a share of the hundreds of millions of rands spent each year by African consumers cannot run more than one business in a township or sell anything except "essential domestic requirements." They also cannot form trading companies, partnerships, financial institutions or wholesale concerns.

31

Every move aimed at self-reliance by Sowetonians in moneymaking is undermined by the government whose policy is "no-black-advancement-and-no-equality" of blacks with whites and the "Bantus" being made to develop separately on their own lines in the tribal Bantustans. To implement its ethnic policy on Soweto traders the government has even directed the formation of ethnic branches of the Chamber of Commerce. Shops are allocated on a tribal basis too!

This move to divide the Johannesburg African Chamber of Commerce on a linguistic basis is one of the methods used by the government Bantu Administration Department to facilitate its transference of African traders from urban areas to the Bantustans. Traders are hounded by BAD officials to move to the homelands. Having moved to the Bantustans the urban traders are not allowed to keep their previous shops nor to return to the urban areas.

Given the tough government restriction on entrepreneurs in Soweto, it is therefore an enigma to the man in the street that there in fact are a handful of men who own more than one business. Such "tycoons" run petrol-filling stations, dry-cleaners, chemists and sell clothing. One such "millionaire" was the first "mayor" of Soweto, chosen under the hateful Urban Bantu Council scheme, who was somehow always at hand, with BAD officials and police, to "negotiate" workers' disputes. Another such Mr. Moneybags once announced in public that he was willing to go to the United Nations to testify that "we Bantus are happy and peaceful living in South Africa under the apartheid regime." Then there is the case of another rich man who owns a butcher shop, and a luxurious, expensively appointed, six-bedroomed three-bathroomed home with "every amenity" on two stands in Dube, Soweto's most affluent suburb. According to a newspaper report Marina and Richard Maponya's dining-room table with twelve chairs has seated many celebrities both local and overseas—Chris and Barbara Barnard, Arthur Ashe, Charles Diggs, the USA Black Congressman, Dorothy Heights, president of the National Council of Negro Women, Laurent Donafologo, Ivory Coast Minister of Foreign Affairs, as well as many British and American consuls. (*Rand Daily Mail* 29/12/75).

Credit

Soweto lives on credit—its future wages are pledged in meeting debts, paying rent and buying food. Some Soweto houses are equipped with a radiogram, a dining room suite, an American kitchen scheme and a refrigerator. These household appliances are bought on hire purchase agreement. Deposit, which is half the price of a purchased item, is required before the buyer can get the required item. Invariably if a buyer does not have enough cash deposit he then trades-in to the shop, at the shop's estimate, property to balance the required deposit. The remainder is paid on weekly or monthly instalments. Sewing machines are promoted. With eye-catching advertisements they tell the Soweto woman that "you can become a highly successful businesswoman by sewing and knitting at home" with a Singer machine or Empisal Knitting machine. These companies offer "free" sewing and knitting lessons with the purchase of a machine.

Nationally known furniture shops are located in predominantly "black spots" of the city—Hoek Street and Noord Street near the Johannesburg Station, West Street near Westgate Station and downtown Eloff Street next to Faraday Station—where black workers commute to and from work every day. These shops are entirely staffed by black workers as shop assistants, credit controllers, cashiers, salesmen, canvassers, demonstrators, clerks, drivers and in certain cases managers and manageresses. Most furniture sold in these shops is of low-quality timber, mass-produced and selling at inflated prices.

Clothing is also bought on credit. The internationally known clothing stores like Tru-Worths and Edwards have exploited to the full the government policy of segregated shopping by opening in the city exclusive shops to cater for black customers only. Tru-Worths opened up a number of branches passing under the special name "Top Centre". The Edwards group opened the well-known Sales House. These shops too are served by a predominantly black staff. Here, low quality clothes are sold to the blacks on hire purchase agreements. Customers who fail to pay their instalments are sent threatening notices of "intent to prosecute if you do not pay within three days." Sales House is notorious for repossessing clothes from customers in default. Even when the clothes are soaking wet, hanging on the line, Sales House agents are known to unpeg and confiscate them. The police often harrass Soweto residents on their way home on Fridays, by stopping them and demanding receipts for any goods they are carrying—to prove they are not stolen.

Racket second-hand car dealers in association with lending clubs make fantastic profits from the black market. They operate by advertising loans available for the purchase of cars. A borrower is required to pay an advance "commitment fee" with his application for a loan. Sometimes he is required to pay a weekly or monthly subscription to the club until the money is enough for the deposit fees of a car. Of course the deposit will be half the price of the car. The club will undertake to pay the balance which the buyer will repay in instalments. Once a car is purchased and delivered to him, the buyer has no power to demand his money back should the car fail to move the following day. Frequently the cars purchased this way can hardly do a fifty kilometre run. Should the subscriber refuse to pay the balance, the club repossesses the car and keeps the money already paid.

The whole system of hire purchase agreement is loaded with abuse. First what happens is that groups of canvassers are driven to Soweto by these various shops. Canvassers carry with them attractive brochures advertising their commodities. The canvassers use very smooth and persuasive language to sell their wares because they earn more money on commission. In a community whose understanding of advertising trappings and whose reading level is low, customers sign contracts out of ignorance, thus purchasing useless and expensive items which are beyond their earnings. Sometimes the customers do not demand copies of the Hire Purchase Agreements and they seldom keep receipts of payments to protect them against excess payment which most shops demand.

Before the shop approves a contract the potential customer is "investigated" to determine his chances of being able to pay the account in full. His employer must vouchsafe his period of employment, wages and reliability. Enquiries about the customer's other possible credit accounts are made from an organisation which keeps credit control records on behalf of the retail stores. The township administrative offices are asked if the potential buyer is a bona fide tenant of a house or hostel and pays his rent regularly. Should the potential customer be of bad standing with any of these concerns his contract is automatically cancelled.

The burden of debt in Soweto is staggering and the pressure of the instalments on furniture, cars, burial insurance and so on unbearable. One can only conclude that those who deal in this type of financing look towards the time when hire purchase instalment payments fall into arrears and the property can be confiscated. This confiscated property is in turn sold to other buyers at original cost prices without deducting the depreciation price value. The black public's purchasing power is thus exploited by the white business world.

Food and Drink

How does a Soweto dweller eat? Unscrupulous trading is rife in Soweto. Customers are overcharged as much as 50% for food items. In a recent investigation by the milk board it was found that customers were overcharged as much as 33% for a litre of milk. This comes as no surprise because the traders are forced to make quick profits since their businesses are not in a favourable competitive market, they do not get mortgages, and have very little chance of investing money in the completely white-dominated economy with all its apartheid curbs.

Generally speaking the African workers prefer to shop in the city where they work. In this era of frozen and refrigerated foods in the city, the people of Soweto have comparatively easy access to average food supplies. But the bitter irony is that the Soweto dwellers have little or no money to buy foodstuffs in the bustling city stores. The nationally known food chains like O.K. Bazaars, Woolworths, Spar and Checkers have not neglected to take advantage of the concentrated purchasing power of black people. Some of these shops have even "bent" apartheid rules by employing blacks as cashiers and salesmen. The "Whites only" signs on the escalators have been removed and black models are used in food advertisements appearing in "non-white" newspapers. But on wages of six rand to ten rand per week how much can the Sowetonian in the barest income bracket spend on food ? Rent and train ticket come first, then food. The agonising pain about apartheid in South Africa is that when white Johannesburg shoppers produce several rand notes to spend on food the African shopper scratches the bottom of his purse for a few cents to buy staple food like mealie-meal, milk, eggs and meat.

The Christian Institute magazine *Pro Veritate* reported that over 1,000 black children aged between seven and fourteen fend for themselves in the Johannesburg streets, daily. They live on what they can beg or steal and often die from the effects of malnutrition and glue-sniffing. They smoke glue to get drunk and stop feeling hungry.

This is the plight of hardworking and exploited black workers.

Where, then, does the money come from to keep the beerhalls and liquor stores busy with customers and thriving with money to finance the wastelands of the Bantustans ? The answer is that the money withheld or diverted for liquor is often, though not always, that which should have been reserved for furniture instalments and burial insurance collectors. It is not money saved, for Soweto workers earn starvation wages. Sowetonians have easy access to the incredible number of liquor stores, beerhalls and bar lounges strategically built near the railway stations and main street intersections. These liquor dens tell the sordid story of an oppressed people lulled into oblivion. To add insult to their dehumanisation the liquor profits extorted out of Sowetonians are used by the Government to finance the development of the Bantustan wastelands.

Sowetonians belong to the most heavily taxed racial group in South Africa. They not only pay the R2·50 annual poll tax levied on Africans but not other races, but those who earn more than R10 a week also have income and homeland tax deductions from their weekly wages. By contributing to the income tax the African worker is subsidising the whole of South Africa's economy from which he does not benefit and by paying the additional homeland tax the African worker is made to finance the development of the Bantustan wastelands. Should he fail to pay tax, he is jailed.

Because of the poverty and also because of the labour regulations, Soweto mothers must work. They are not encouraged to stay at home with their infants, for the raison d'etre of the townships is that the inhabitants are there solely to sell their labour and normal family life is not part of the plan. Nor, owing to their man's low wages, can Soweto mothers afford to stay at home.

Child Care

Imagine at the crack of dawn the African women, many with two or three children in tow, one of which may be carried on the back, leaving for their work in the city. Food for the day may be carried on their heads or on a free arm. Should there be a granny in the area, or a jobless woman, such women are forced to look after their neighbours' children because of the shortage of nursery schools. This baby care is done illegally and there is a grave shortage of grannies because "superfluous appendages" are not allowed by law to live in Soweto.

I remember as a toddler we dreaded being shunted from house to house because of the shortages of grannies. When there were no grannies available, our mothers were forced to leave us locked alone in a room. They would remove anything dangerous, leaving us with a plate of mealie pap, a mug of water and a chamber pot. Peeping through the drawn curtains and closed windows with window bars was the only enjoyable game. We did it in turns. Otherwise we had fights, cried and slept. Should, on return, our mother hear of any fighting amongst us, we got a good hiding—all over the body. By the age of six our parents regarded us as responsible. We could be left with a house key so as to unlock the house to go to the toilet or to go out and play. You were "bad luck", as we said if you had a baby sister or a baby brother because no key would be left with you. Baby was your first responsibility. When left alone like this, days used to drag and drag on and on. You would cry for your mother until you fell asleep. Most times mother returned when you were out for the count. By this time, if it was in winter, there was no chance of going out to play.

We girls were taught at a very early age to wash dishes and pots. You stood on a chair to wash dishes on the table, or you put the basin on the floor. At six you were able to make the fire in the coalstove and run to the shops to buy an item your mother wanted. Invariably the shop errands were done two or four times because on your return from the previous "shopping" your mother had found the coins she had hidden somewhere in the house or had successfully borrowed a few coins from the "auntie" next door and now she needed onions or curry powder to add flavour to that meagre piece of meat you bought. I remember how our mothers warned us to cover the food items we had gone to buy because should the next door children see it they would tell their moms. Then a few minutes later you would hear a knock on the door, from the child who saw what you had gone to buy. After greeting you all, he would say: "My mother has sent me to come and ask if you, Ma Sikakane, can please be kind and borrow her a slice of onions, or a few teaspoons of salt, or a few teaspoons of tea leaves, or a cup of sugar or a big tin of mealie-meal."

"My mother" the boy would add, "has nothing in the house and she has just received a stranger." (Visitors were always called strangers in the location). "She will pay you back when she gets paid."

The borrowing of candles, sticks of matches, cooking oil, soap and coal were commonest in the location. Neighbours saw to it that they exchanged smiles all the time because when at loggerheads borrowing ceased.

With both parents away at work, the only day in the week we enjoyed was Sunday because our mother was at home. She would wake up early to clean the house thoroughly, do the washing of clothes, look at your body to see if you washed it clean during the course of the week. It was the only day when you could talk to your mother cheerfully and get a nice reply. Sunday was the only day to wear your best dress and go to church or visit a relative and have the best meal with vegetables. I grew up knowing that vegetables were for Sundays only.

Before I started schooling my mother had stopped working in the city where she was employed at a clothing factory. She could no longer bear having to shunt us from house to house in search of childminders. We were always falling sick because of inadequate care and were becoming less affectionate to others. As my mother explained to us when we were older: "I felt that if I did not stop work, I would lose my children." By "losing" her children she meant several things, like us growing up headstrong because of lack of motherly care, us becoming chronically sick because of inadequate food and dying because we were left in the hands of untrained and unloving women.

Life was tough for us children. In the location there were too many cases of children who died of injuries like being accidentally scalded with hot water or burnt by the braziers, or suffering from infectious diseases. Moreover our mothers gave us doses of castor oil at the slightest cough and tummy-ache. "Castor oil will soothe your throat and clear your tummy of the bile," we were told. We hated the stuff and vomited it often.

My Childhood

My mother's decision to leave work was not an easy one because she had to work to supplement my father's meagre earnings. At the time my father was working for the South African Institute of Race Relations. In a country where there is plenty of sunshine, it was a classic demonstration of poverty to find that in each tenement washing was hung up at night before the stove because we had no change of clothes. We girls were always shy to bend before the boys because our panties were always full of holes. Some were mended so often that you would forget the original material and colour.

Having stopped factory work, my mother became a dressmaker in the location. At that time she was permitted to stay at home without being a registered worker, as the wife of J. M. Sikakane, a "Section Tenner". To protect herself against being prosecuted as an illegal dressmaker, she took out an annual hawker's licence. Later such licences became hard to get for self-employed persons like her. They cost R15. By being a dressmaker, she designed, cut and sewed dresses for children and women in the location. Customers either brought their own material or she bought her own to make the garments. We helped her sell her own garments by calling from house to house.

In the 1950's my sister and I enjoyed selling the dresses because at the time the locations were being expanded. We were fascinated by the new "belt system" of building houses. Foundations were laid first, for a series of houses, then concrete floors. Concrete walls en bloc were constructed on the ground, then lifted

37

up with huge suspension belts, ending with asbestos roofs being nailed on them. Noisy zinc doors were installed at the front and back of a building, these were accompanied by two windows on each side. But as the locations were being expanded at a phenomenal speed, with the single-sex male hostels built too, these adventurous exploits were stopped by my mother. It was no longer safe for children to wander around on their own—even if they were selling dresses.

My mother's dressmaking business was by no means a success. She had to charge uncompetitive prices, the customers paid by instalments and some would "disappear" before the account was fully paid. Others lost jobs and had no money to pay. Sometimes if she arrived at a house late for collection, that is after the customer had cleared other debts, she would be told to call next weekend or month-end. There were times when her knock would be answered by a customer's child, who would say to her "My mother said I should say to anyone who calls that she has gone out"—meaning she is hiding in the next room because she has no money to pay the debts.

While my mother was busy sewing, other African women were standing on their feet doing "madam's" washing. Those were the days before the washing-machine had been invented. The clothes of the white families were washed by the hands of the African women. The "washerwomen" would leave home at dawn heading for the white residential areas, collect the clothes, making them into a round bundle with a sheet or bedspread used as a bag. The African woman would then carry it on her head into the less congested mid-morning trains running back to the locations. So during the course of a bright sunny day, it would be the madam's family clothes hanging on the line.

Children's Games

We children had household work to do first after coming back from school. We were always in a hurry to finish it so as to go out and play in the streets. The work entailed washing pots and dishes, removing the ash from the stove, and laying the fire, cleaning the house and polishing the floors and "stoep" (veranda) —a favourite chore because we got personal satisfaction in shining the stoeps brightest "so that at night you could pick up a needle lying on the floor." The popular floor and stoep colours were black and red followed by green. The speed in which the household work was finished depended largely on how many children did it in a house. On returning home from work, parents had to find the work done or else the belt was very much at hand.

When we had a chance to play, the common games were consistent with our standard of living. They were the stone, empty tins and single ball games.

One of the most popular games was that of empty tins built into a pyramid. This game was played by two teams of variable numbers. The main player would aim a tennis ball at the tin pyramid. On making a hit the tins fell a-scatter. The thrower's team ran to rebuild the pyramid while the opposition ran after the ball, picked it up, threw it to the principal fielder, who in turn must hit any member of the building team before the pyramid was completed. Should the pyramid be constructed before a hit, it's a game. The winning team would jump around in jubilation.

This game was most popular because up to 20 children could participate using one ball only. Another game was that of drawing on the ground opposite pairs of circles or squares big enough for one foot. Then, hopping, you would kick a stone around the circles. You were out if the stone missed the next circle, or if when hopping your foot touched the line of a circle.

Many Soweto children spend their lives in the street. Schooling is not compulsory for Africans in South Africa, nor is it free as it is for whites. Many children never reach the classroom at all and of those who do a high proportion drop out before they have completed a primary course.

Education in Soweto

The educational system in Soweto, like that of all African children in South Africa, has been planned by the Nationalist regime to retard the progress of the African people in general. It is designed to create barriers in their development, to humiliate and discourage them. It is planned to make money out of the Blacks as a subservient labour force. The twenty years of "Bantu Education" have attempted to produce mentally retarded African graduates who cannot think beyond their repressed Blackness; after all since Blacks are inferior they cannot become fully responsible leaders and citizens of the South African community!

In Soweto, a community where the population is being reduced and family life discouraged, it comes as no surprise that the very undesirable polluted educational system is limited by the authorities.

Pupils are enrolled according to ethnic groupings in the few primary, secondary and high schools. To ensure that a limited number of pupils enrol in Soweto schools the government has introduced a system whereby each pupil must produce a registration card which is notoriously known to Sowetonians as "a pink card." In it the local superintendent states that a pupil's name is on a registered house permit. Those children whose names do not appear on a house permit are not issued with the pink cards; thus they are refused enrolment at school. A birth certificate is no longer a criterion for a child's registration at school.

Parents pay for the school fees, books and uniforms. Through a levy included in the monthly house rentals they also subsidise the building of schools. The levy is 38c a month. Africans are the only racial group in South Africa which contributes directly towards the cost of building schools. The costs for the other races come from the general revenue.

The overall academic performance is poor because of the shortage of teachers and overcrowding. Double-sessions, dubbed the "hot-system" by Sowetonians were introduced by the Bantu Education Department to increase the number of children who could be admitted into existing primary schools without incurring extra capital costs. Pupils read for three hours in each session and the same teacher takes both sessions. Another factor is that pupils start school in Soweto at the age of seven compared to five for whites. African pupils have to spend two years in the "pre-primary" classes called sub-standards A and B whereas white pupils get enrolled in Standard 1 from the beginning. African pupils also have to spend a year in Standard 6, a grade which is not done by pupils of other races who transfer to secondary school at this stage. Therefore Africans pupil in primary school spend three extra years compared to pupils of other races.

The rate of school "push-outs" is high because of the whole degrading educational system. Soweto has no university, no technical college, no commercial college and no teacher training college. Soweto parents are eager to educate their children. Those who can afford it send them to boarding schools situated in rural areas. Disturbed by the soaring number of "push-outs" roaming Soweto streets, early in 1973, an Urban Bantu Councillor, Mr. Peter Lengene, decided to call the police to "collect" the juveniles, hand them over to their parents and order that the children be sent to school.

The police responded quickly to this call. The youths were "collected" in pick-up police vans and locked up in cells at the police station. Those aged sixteen and above who had not yet obtained passes were prosecuted, those who had passes but were not working were all sent to the Bantustan transit camps as they were "undesirable idling Bantus." The under-sixteens were ordered to return to their parents and attend school. They were required to report to the police station every day on their way to and from school. They were made to sign a police register to prove that they were at school. A Soweto child is thus subjected to police control at a very tender age even though the law does not provide for free and compulsory education or means to keep an African child at school.

The vast majority of blacks do not become literate, judged by the fact that most leave school before standard 2 and only 31% of the total at school complete standard 2. Therefore almost 70% of the already meagre resources allocated to black education are being virtually wasted.

My Schooldays

When I started schooling in 1950, the apartheid regime which took office in 1948 was already legislating its new policy and moving towards its implementation. When the regime took power it did so under the slogan "swart gevaar"—that is "the black danger." One of its primary aims was to provide for separate

Entrance to Soweto. In the background a power station serving white Johannesburg. (Photo by John Seymour)

The Soweto landscape. (Photo by John Seymour)

Johannesburg City. (Photo by Abisag Tüllman)

Pimville, the oldest part of Soweto.   (Photo by John Seymour)

In some parts of Soweto there exists only one water tap for every block of houses.
(Photo by John Seymour)

Black commuters travel 3rd class.   (Photo by John Seymour)

Outside a Soweto school.   (Photo by John Seymour)

A standard four-room Soweto home. (*Photo by Abisag Tüllman*)

Backyard toilets for each pair of Soweto houses. (*Photo by John Seymour*)

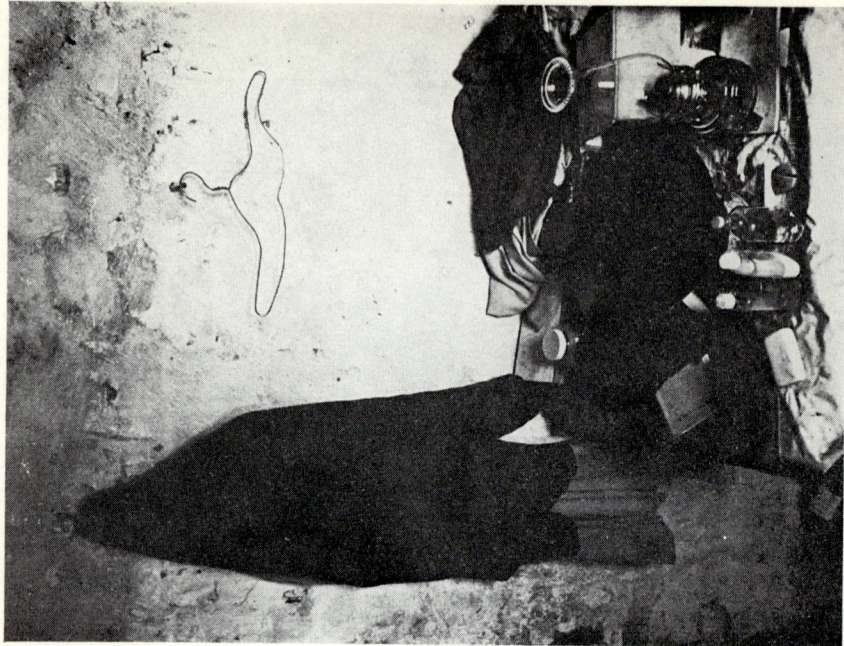

Inside a Soweto home. (Photo by John Seymour)

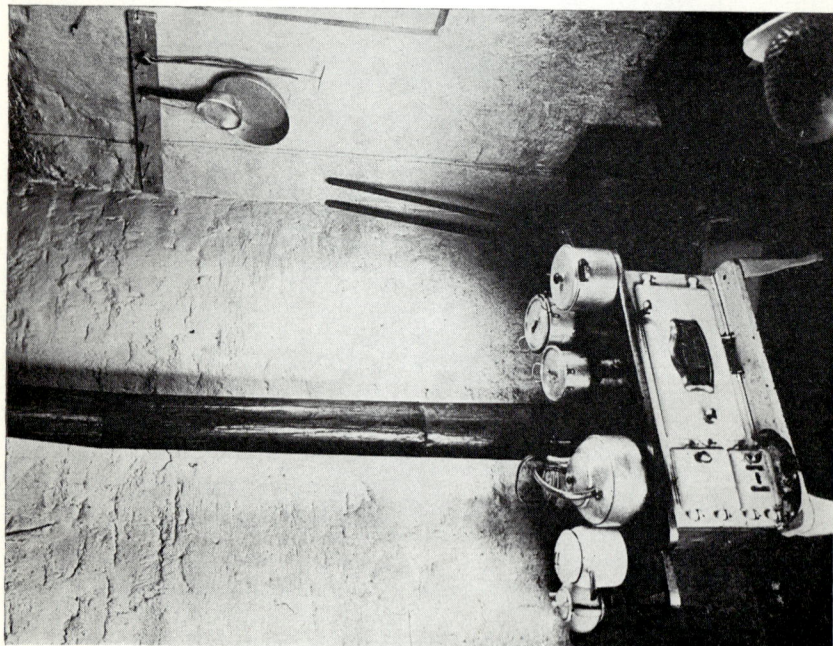

Kitchen facilities in Soweto home. (Photo by John Seymour)

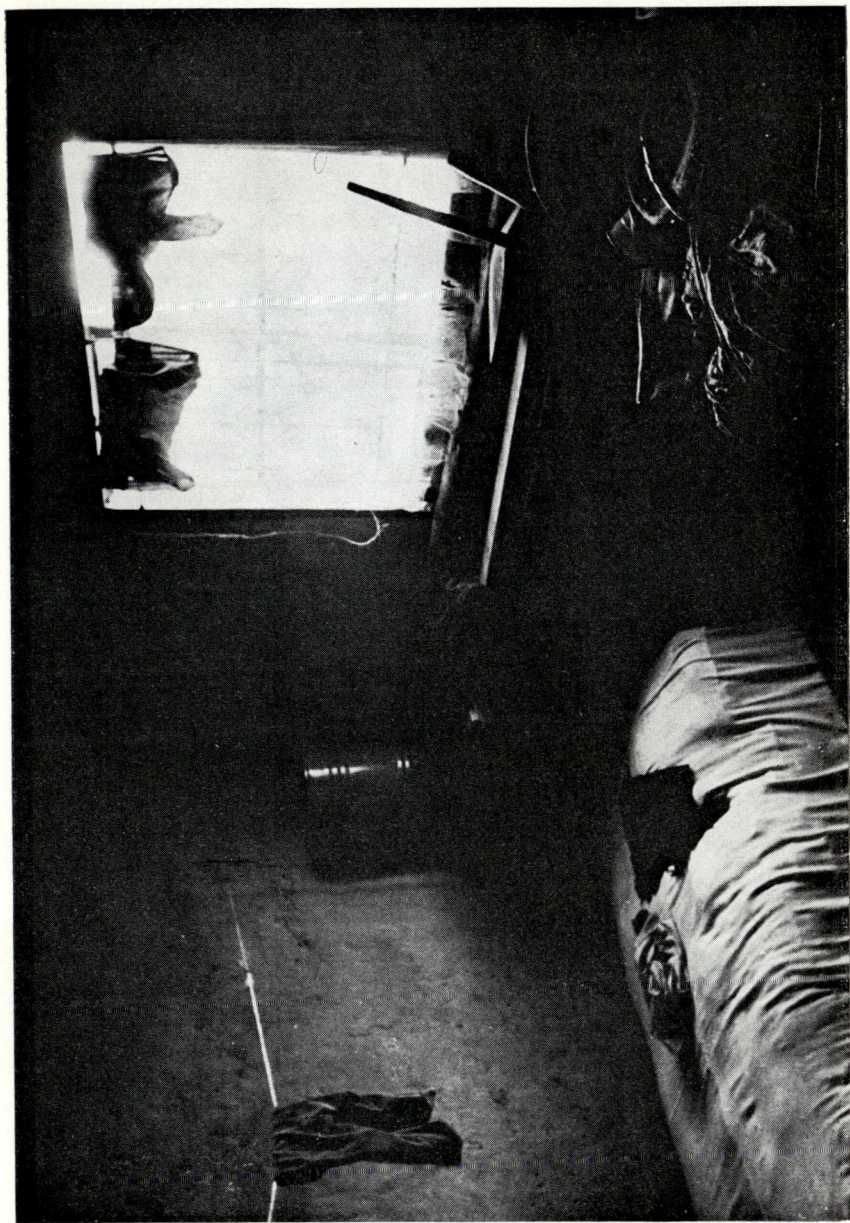

Bedroom in Soweto home. (Photo by John Seymour)

The author with Shanthie Naidoo.

native education. 1954 was the year of the formal switch to Bantu Education for all African children. I remember hearing our parents talking about it, saying "the Boers were wanting to indoctrinate African children into being perpetual slaves of the white man." I was then a pupil at a primary school run by the Anglican Church, and that famous priest Trevor Huddleston was in charge of the parish whose school I attended.

The African community was up in arms against Bantu Education. It was the talk of the nation. We as children were made to understand what the fight was all about. The Anglican Church announced that rather than submit it would close all its schools, responding to a call by the African National Congress of South Africa (ANC). Therefore, the school I attended was closed. Several "cultural clubs"—unlicensed schools—were started by the Congress, but were not enough to cater for thousands of children. Moreover the government warned that children who were not at state schools would be expelled and a fine of £50 imposed on unlicensed schools.

The closure of church schools meant that we as children had nothing to do during the course of the day. Since we understood why that was done we did not mind, but then we began to enjoy playing truant when our parents were away at work. This posed a problem. My father decided to send me and my eldest sister to Durban to live with my grandfather. Here there was a private Roman Catholic School which, because of a possible loophole in the legal interpretation of the Bantu Education Act, could delay introducing the new racial syllabus. I must say my sister and I were fortunate to be among the tiny fraction of children enrolled in such schools. Not long after, the Roman Catholic school also had to introduce Bantu Education. In the following year at this school, I had the first taste of an apartheid education.

At Clermont Township, my grandpa the Rev. Sikakane was participating in full ANC activities. He chaired the local ANC branch meetings and was appointed ANC chaplain for Natal. It was during this period that I first became aware of the national character of the struggle against the apartheid regime and white domination.

One event which is always in my mind is the day in 1958 when I helped my grandfather prepare a dinner for the Natal ANC members who were in the Treason Trial. They were to meet at my grandfather's home before flying to Pretoria for the Treason Trial. I shook hands with Chief Lutuli, who was then ANC national president, Mr. M. B. Yengwa, Natal ANC secretary, and Dorothy Nyembe, the woman now serving 15 years in gaol in South Africa. They were all so dignified and unperturbed at having to go and face a trial which could have cost their lives. They lifted the clenched fist salute and the thumbs-up as they sang "Nkosi' sikelela i Afrika" (the African national anthem) before they left my grandfather's home. In 1956, my grandfather had been among the Natal ANC delegation which went to the Kliptown Congress which adopted the Freedom Charter, a historic occasion.

In 1958, I finished primary school and my parents decided to send me to boarding school. The reasons were that my widowed grandfather was growing old, and since I had reached 14 my parents felt it was not safe to let me attend a day school because of the high rate of juvenile delinquency, school drop-outs, crime and girl pregnancies. My parents had to work harder and deprive themselves of essentials to afford the boarding school fees. While in boarding school in 1960, I received the news of my grandfather's detention under the State of Emergency. The husband of one of our teachers, Mrs. E. Yengwa, had also been detained. It was the same M. B. Yengwa who had been acquitted at the Treason Trial. Mrs. Yengwa took it upon herself to explain to us what the State of Emergency meant, and that African people would not be intimidated by jails in the fight for freedom.

To me, Mrs. Yengwa's brave words were a source of encouragement; the struggle had to be continued. The detainees spent more than six months in jail. Immediately thereafter the ANC was banned and it went underground. We students got organised into secret cells of the African Student Association (ASA). I remember how one night at boarding school we were addressed by the late Ernest Gallo who had been "smuggled into the campus."

It was at boarding school in 1960 that I turned 16—a "doomsday" instead of a happy birthday because I had to carry a pass, a "reference book" I had to carry every day of my life or else face a gaol sentence. I was at boarding school when the passbook was issued instantly to me and 300 other girls. We had not been informed, we were taken out in small groups for finger prints and instant photographing by the Bantu Affairs officials, who had set up a mobile station in the college grounds. We who were politically active failed to organise a protest. The government had adopted very stringent measures to see to it that African women above 15 years carried the passes after its first attempts had failed. Stated in the reference book were all my names, where I was born and date of birth, who my father was and where he lived and worked.

In 1961, I had a break from boarding school and enrolled for first-year matric at Orlando High School, Soweto. There were two first-year matric classes, with more than 70 pupils in each class. Here at Orlando High School I experienced what it meant to be in a classroom in which almost all pupils were without textbooks. That handful of students who possessed books had to share them with the rest of the class. The only time a pupil was left to his own book was when all pupils who had no books were ordered out of school by the principal. Ordered out to go and find books, invariably many pupils would never return, or some did with one or two books, others with explanations that books would be forthcoming at the end of the month—after their parents' pay-day.

Because of the heavy workload on teachers, exercise work hardly ever got marked. Lots of time was wasted on music practice for competitions which fell outside the syllabus, because Africans were supposed to be so good at music! Added bitter experience came when pupils were refused admission to a class because they were not in full school uniform.

Bantu Education meant being taught of a tribal identity. In their history books, it meant that the white man "discovered" the "savage" African and civilised him. The derogatory word "Bantu" was used instead of African.

It meant being taught that our national heroes like Tshaka and Hintsa were brutal murderers yet they were African patriots who fought against the white invasion of our country. One such book full of distortion of the South African history was written by Fowler and Smith. We dubbed it "Foul and Smither."

It meant being taught that the white man is superior to a black man. Above all it meant the unquestionable acceptance of the philosophy of apartheid.

When I came to write the matric (university entrance) examination in December 1963, the Tribal Colleges (universities) had already been opened. At our boarding school we were strongly opposed to these tribal institutions, so a big number of us refused to go and study there. We chose to go and work or enter other professions like nursing.

I had always enjoyed reading and writing so I looked for a job in journalism. First I had to comply with the pass laws by registering with a labour office.

Registering for Work

Under the notorious Pass Laws (Section 10) there are four categories of lawful residents in any African urban area: those who were:
(a) born there
(b) have worked for 10 or lived for 15 years under certain conditions
(c) are the wife or child under 16 of person qualified under (a)
(d) have work permit and accommodation.
Only the first three convey any residence rights.

I was a Section Tenner, having been born in Soweto, and being the daughter of a man who also qualified. But my pass had been issued to me while at boarding school in Natal.

At the labour bureau I had my first brush with a white labour official, who maintained that it was illegal to have been issued with a reference book in Natal for a Jo'burg Section Ten. I was just like one of those "educated Bantu female crooks." He wanted proof. The only proof I thought of was my father's pass book. I went back home. In the evening I explained the problem to my dad, he agreed that his "dompass" would be the only authorised proof. But then he did not have time to accompany me to the labour office the next day. He had to be at work. He could not dream of giving me his pass in case anything happened to it. Besides it would mean he would be arrested by the cops if he failed to produce it. Finally he decided he would risk it and gave me his pass. I was not to leave it at the labour office. On the following day, with his pass and mine deeply buried in my bosom, I ran most of the two-mile distance to the labour office. When my turn came, I showed the labour officer my father's "dompass." In it was stated where he was born and that he was a registered house tenant and employee. The official took down notes and gave me the stinker back. Despite this documentary proof, he had to check with Pretoria before granting me permission to register as an employed "Bantu" female. I waited for three months for such clearance. You can imagine all my anxiety in case I was endorsed out of Jo'burg. Finally I got the notorious labour stamp of a Section Tenner. I was officially a desirable "Bantu" female.

I then had to report to the "Bantu Female Section" of the Non-European Affairs Labour Office in the City, for a medical examination and registration as a worker. There were hundreds of African women in the labour pen. I had left home after 8 a.m. and on arrival found I had no chance that morning of being processed through. I returned home. The following day I was in the train at 6 a.m. and it took the whole "labour" day to be processed. Imagine hundreds of African women sitting on benches of the labour pen. They are called to the offices in groups. Once inside their "dompasses" are taken by an official. The women are told to sit down again. As time goes on their names are called one by one. When your turn comes you go to the official who asks you your names, where you were born and on what date. She pages through the passbook as you answer. More questions follow. Your father's names, where he was born, where he is employed and as what. Your home address. Then she goes to a filing system from which your family's house file is removed. She checks your answers and then gets forms where she writes information about where you are being employed, as what and at what salary. You are then given two cards to be filled by your prospective employer and one to be sent back to the labour office.

I was to start newspaper work with *The World*, a paper run for an African readership in Johannesburg. The clerk wrote in the passbook that I was employed as a "filing clerk" instead of as a "reporter." African women are not allowed by law and convention to do skilled jobs like reporting and typing. In certain establishments they might get away with it, provided no white person complains. When I said my salary was to be R9 a week, she remarked that it was too much! After she had finished with the registration, she told me where to go next. It was to a room where women were undressing, and going in turn to lie on beds standing in open cubicles. I did likewise when my turn came. The doctor who examined me was only interested in my genitalia. Having found it clean, she gave me a medical clearance.

It is in this labour office that urban African women are registered as workers and screened for any possible violation of the influx control regulations. On that day alone, I saw countless women leaving the offices openly sobbing because they had been "endorsed out". It is also in these offices that you find jobs for domestic and nannies widely advertised. All jobs to serve white women in their homes at very low wages, or menial jobs such as tea-makers and cleaners in city offices where in addition African women are forced during their own lunchtime to do personal shopping for white workers.

I worked for the *World* for 2½ years and in that time came across many instances of the harsh way apartheid affected people in the urban areas. But as a reporter on the *World* I was not happy because a white man, who was the News Editor and Editorial Director, wanted crime stories and other sensational stories only. We had to hunt around the Soweto streets to select the most gruesome accounts of murder stories. The injustices of the apartheid system were not to appear in this newspaper although critical leaders and articles were printed.

The Insecurity of Apartheid

One of the most dehumanizing feature stories I was ever assigned to was that of the marriages of old-age folks whose homes were being shut down in Soweto and in the Katlhehong Township of Germiston. The News Director seemed to be fascinated by the fact that men and women whose ages varied from 70 to 100 years were getting married. The truth, I discovered as I was interviewing these "amorous" couples, was that the decisions to marry came because they were terrified to part from communities they had been born in and lived all their lives. They were being moved to the Bantustans and they were selected for these areas according to the ethnic spelling of their surnames. For example, an aged person with a Zulu surname, even if she did not speak a word of Zulu, was to be "repatriated" to the KwaZulu Bantustan. Terrified of being repatriated alone to strange places, these aged persons arranged marriages of future companionship. The cruelty of the "repatriation scheme" was that the government regarded the urban African aged as "superfluous appendages" no longer useful to serve the white man in the City.

I wrote the story pointing out the facts behind these sudden marriages of men and women of 70 to 100 years and the fact that the newly-weds would spend their honeymoons and life forever after in the desolate Bantustans. When I read the newspaper in the afternoon, it had only a group picture and caption of the "Happy Newly-weds." I felt angry and disgusted.

There were many other ways in which the web of laws and regulations created problems for people. In early 1966, I was expecting a baby, and for personal reasons and social ones I was not in a hurry to get married. The social factors against marriage were that had we got married we had no chance of renting a house of our own. Families on the housing list had reached the 660,000 mark. Marriage would have meant moving to a four-roomed bathroomless house where a family of five lived. Besides, my man was Tswana-speaking and the apartheid state was busy rehousing Soweto residents on an ethnic basis.

In Soweto alone there are thousands of one-parent families. Some are separated from their spouses by the influx control laws; some are widows—men are the main victims of murder; and some are local women who have become pregnant by those thousands of migrant single-sex hostel dwellers. However, the community has come to terms with its plight. It does not look down on pregnant unmarried women and their subsequent offspring. In addition, the rigours of apartheid laws have so disrupted normal African life that the dignity of marriage has lost its deeper meaning in the eyes of the youth of the ghetto.

A critic might ask why so many illegitimate babies ? or what about contraception ? When the introduction of "the pill" hit the world headlines, and the nations of the world were advised about the advantages of population control and family planning, in South Africa the apartheid regime saw "the pill" as "god-sent" to limit the rise of the African population, not as a means of spacing children in a family. An opposite stand was adopted in regard to the white population.

The regime openly called for the production of more white babies and offered incentives to white mothers. It was a government Minister of Bantu Administration who made the call and his name was Botha, so the press termed the plea "the Botha babies plea." The African community responded as any "threatened nation" would: it continued to produce more babies. Apartheid is a life-denying and indeed murderous system, and our response was a determination to live and resist.

It so happened that at that time my parents had decided to divorce. This decision was the most agonising for the family in terms of the requirements of Section 10 of the Bantu Urban Areas Act, which forbade "single" persons to be registered tenants of a house. My parents had been on judicial separation for a long time so as to avoid turning each member of the family in single-sex hostel dwellers. My father had "illegally" moved out of the house and was an "illegal" sub-tenant in various houses in Soweto. He was tired of being caught up in the blackjack raids and had also met a woman who he wanted to marry. He was at this time a lecturer at Witwatersrand University.

This was the most excruciating time for all of us. My mother was not thinking of remarrying, she wanted to continue living with her children. Both my youngest brothers were pupils at local schools. Eventually, in 1968 my parents took the risk and got divorced. My mother and we remained in the house under constant threat of eviction. Even today, my mother, two brothers and two children still live under the same threat. I do not need to add that there were times when my mother would be summoned to the superintendent's office where such a possibility of being evicted was put to her. In Soweto it is common practice to bribe the Authorities for such matters as house permits.

Medical Services

While pregnant I attended ante-natal care at a local clinic where each pregnant woman is only examined once—on her very first visit—by a doctor. Only women with serious complications are examined by the doctor more than once.

The only maternity hospital for African women in the whole of Johannesburg is at Baragwanath. It is reserved for pregnant women who work as domestic servants and who live in the domestic quarters of the white residential areas or in the single-sex hostels. This is done for two reasons, first the apartheid regime would not tolerate the birth of black babies in white areas, although by accident some babies decide to come before time, and are thus born at a white man's premises. Secondly, it is done so as to record babies who are not supposed to qualify for the Section 10 permit because their mothers in the hostels do not qualify, babies who have to be sent to the homelands as soon as their mothers get discharged.

When my contractions started one of my brothers ran a distance of almost two miles to a local clinic to call a midwife. He returned before the jeep carrying the midwife had arrived. After detecting that I was in the first labour stage, the midwife left, explaining that she had other deliveries to contend with. The jeep brought her back after hours. Because my labour was long, the baby was born the following day just as the midwife had been biting her fingernails anxious that the jeep call immediately so that I could be rushed to Baragwanath Hospital as a complicated case. Dropping a midwife at each call, the jeep drove to other calls where midwives were in attendance, and then moved to the clinic to return them, or sped to the hospital with a complicated case. In Soweto, it is common for mothers to die while giving birth and to give birth to stillborn babies because the midwife and jeep were too late to call. The midwives work under tremendous pressure. Besides, those two-to four-roomed crowded houses are not hygienic as places of delivery, neither are they equipped with emergency units.

In general in Soweto there is an acute shortage of medical services although the people pay for these facilities through a rent levy and fees paid on receiving medical treatment. There are less than ten clinics in Soweto. These clinics are mostly staffed by retired white doctors because of the poor working conditions and the disparity in salary scale for black and white doctors. African doctors are paid less than what is earned by white doctors. African nurses also earn low wages. These clinics treat minor ailments like 'flu, cuts, stab wounds, burns and backaches. Patients used to pay 50c (fifty cents) for each treatment, mothers a R5 (five rand) fee for pre-natal treatment. The clinics also serve as filters for Baragwanath Hospital, the only hospital catering for Africans in the whole of Johannesburg.

A number of private doctors, African, White, Indian and Coloured, have private surgeries in Soweto. The African doctors are being threatened with removal to the homelands. All these private practitioners make a lucrative financial business by charging high fees unrelated to medical treatment.

When the Transvaal Provincial Council took over the running of Soweto clinics in April 1974 from the Johannesburg City Council it reintroduced racial salary scales for doctors. For a few months, the Council had been paying black and white doctors equally but the Provincial Council reduced the salary of black doctors by R2,000 and the Transvaal Administrator accused the City Council of having done a "dangerous thing" in raising the pay of black doctors to white levels.

A survey among 12,000 Soweto schoolchildren showed the highest known incidence in the world of rheumatic heart disease, a potentially crippling disorder which if unchecked, leads to serious heart damage and death. The result of this survey was reported by Dr. Margaret McLaren who organised the survey project on behalf of the cardiac unit of the University of the Witwatersrand. She reported that "Rheumatic heart disease is a socio-economic related condition and is therefore largely preventable. Overcrowding has been proved to be the single most important socio-economic factor involved. Nutritional factors are also associated with rheumatic heart disease." Dr. McLaren's findings show that the incidence of rheumatic heart disease in Soweto is nearly eighteen times greater than anywhere else in the world.

A survey published in the Medical Journal in 1965 on behalf of the National Nutrition Research Institute found that "at least 80% of schoolgoing children from African households in Pretoria suffer from malnutrition or undernutrition." Between 75 and 85% of households had an income lower than the minimum needed for basic expenses. This malnutrition is usually associated with rural poverty in underdeveloped countries: in South Africa it exists in the heart of a rich agricultural and industrial nation.

South Africa is very famous too with medical visitors. In comparison with other parts of the African continent medical facilities are well developed (although a marked difference exists between those for white and non-white). Johannesburg shares in this constant stream of visitors from all parts of the world and an invariable part of their tour is a visit to Baragwanath Hospital situated on the outskirts of Soweto. Being the principal hospital for Soweto it never fails to impress, particularly when it is indicated that this hospital serves more than half a million people and is in fact their first and only hope of medical treatment.

Visitors invariably leave with an impression of a large busy progressive hospital coping admirably with an intolerable work load and giving the Africans a surprisingly good service. It is only by working in this hospital and experiencing over a long period its difficulties and problems that a true appreciation of its achievements and failings can be seen.

My husband Ken spent ten months working there fulltime and thus obtained an intimate working knowledge of it. In his words Baragwanath Hospital can truly be described as a phenomenon. Originally built during the second world war as a tuberculosis hospital for troops being repatriated, it takes its name from the airfield and area nearby. It presents an open single storey construction sprawling over a large area. Estimates of the patients present have always been a popular hobby with the medical staff but the official figure for beds is 2,500. However, as later remarks will show, there are always more patients than beds and the usual estimates for patients range between 2,500 and 3,000. The hospital deals with every form of medical complaint with the exception of eye diseases for which there is a separate hospital nearby. The full range of medical, surgical, obstetric, gynaecological and children's facilities are provided. Moreover, there are specialities within the large subdivisions, e.g. Neurosurgery, Chest Surgery,

Orthopaedics and Urology within the section of Surgery. In medicine there are specialists in renal diseases and chest and cardiac disorders. Although serving mainly Soweto the facilities are such that consultants bring patients from all parts of the Reef if they require complex procedures or investigations, and also from other parts of South Africa.

The Specialist Units are moderately well developed at Baragwanath, but there is no doubt that the bulk of the work load in, for example, surgery, falls on the five general surgical units. It is here that the major defect of the hospital is demonstrated. Each of these surgical units is headed by one full-time consultant surgeon with a varying number of junior staff. Each is in fact grossly overworked and every fifth day deals with all the surgical emergencies for a twenty-four hour period for the whole of Soweto. The full-time consultant is aided at times by a part-time man who may or may not contribute substantially to the work of the unit. These five consultants contrast vividly with the more than eighty surgeons in private practice who serve the half million white population in Johannesburg. That each surgical unit functions efficiently is entirely due to the constant goodwill and energy of the consultant surgeon in charge.

That the work load is heavy will be seen from the admission figures. A quiet night means the admission of 10-20 patients, a moderate one 30-40 patients, but a heavy admission night meant upwards of 50 patients. Road accidents and fighting make up a large part of this admission figure. Most of the staff of the surgical team on duty don't expect to sleep at any time while on emergency duty. Frequently the staff have to work the next morning up to 10, 12 noon or even later.

The next obvious defect regards beds. Although having such a large number of beds, having to put patients on the floor is a common occurrence. On one occasion Ken recalls that for a period of six weeks he always had no less than six female patients and sometimes more accommodated on the floor and the same was true of the male ward. For a hospital which deals extensively with surgical cases this was without question an extremely serious situation. Several times patients could not receive adequate treatment because they did not have a bed to lie on. Not that the consultant staff acquiesced in this situation. Frequent requests were made for the number of beds to be increased. On one occasion a new unit of 50 beds was built. It made almost no difference and there were still many floor patients. The underlying reason was blatantly political. To increase the facilities too much, it was said, would be to encourage the African to believe that he had a permanent place in Johannesburg. Such ideas could never be encouraged. It was always a cause for thought to drive home from Baragwanath past the beautiful brand new Strydom Hospital for whites just opened but only 50% used (shortage of nurses it was said, though in 1976 the position was still the same) and think of the patients one had just left behind lying on the floor.

Bed shortage has other undesirable effects. There was always a tendency to discharge patients too soon to make way for the inevitable wave of new admissions.

This in several instances led to very serious results. Also admissions for non-urgent operations must obviously suffer. A regular waiting list of admissions is almost impossible. Hence it is found that Baragwanath at least on the surgical side is ninety per cent a hospital for emergencies.

The attitude of most of the white medical staff was on the whole admirable. Dealing with an enormous work load they managed to maintain enthusiasm and willingness to a remarkable degree. However there were exceptions. Unfortunately it was these which on many occasions could undo much of the good work done by others. Some, and one of the consultants Ken worked for was one, displayed such a derogatory attitude to their African patients that it bordered on the unethical. Such doctors exemplified to a large extent the racial tensions underlying South Africa's apartheid system. To them the patients were little better than animals and their treatment of them could be brutal to the extent that it was painful to observe.

With some doctors their contempt for the African was obvious in their attitude and conversation. Some were not so subtle and would take delight in patients dying saying that there were then fewer for the (Nationalist) Government to worry about. This would at times be stated in humorous terms as part of general light hearted banter making a serious discussion of these views very difficult.

Baragwanath has an all African nursing staff, with one exception. The Senior Matron was (and always will be) white. Thus the most privileged position was denied even the most capable African.

Although Baragwanath is the principal hospital for Soweto it is not the only one. In the centre of Johannesburg was a small wing of the General Hospital called the Non-European Hospital. With only about 40 beds it could not deal with more than a minute fraction of the work load. It was maintained (much to the annoyance and frustration of the Nationalist Government) for the express purpose of dealing with those Africans injured in the centre of the city or who took ill while working as domestic servants in the densely populated white areas of the city. Its subsidiary purpose and the one which was always forwarded when the regular closure threat loomed was that it served as a teaching unit for the Medical School. Its presence was always a bone of contention and a shocking danger to patients. Being so small it could not deal completely with many patients. The vast majority who were taken there received only emergency and first aid treatment, and were then, and this is where the danger lay, transferred to Baragwanath—10 miles away! Not that the patients were transferred as and when their condition permitted. This would at least have been logical and safe. Patients would be admitted during the day, given emergency treatment and about 10 p.m. they would all be loaded on to a bus or into ambulances and transferred to Baragwanath, with little or no regard to their condition and more concern about the availability of transport. Thus while on emergency duty at the other end one could look forward with certainty to the arrival of the bus full of patients—wounds bleeding, drips run dry, sometimes infusion bottles broken, inadequately splinted fractures, all because the white man decrees that Africans must not stay overnight in hospitals in "white areas." Such a practice runs counter to all the principles of emergency surgery and humanitarianism. It also meant a further burden on the already overloaded surgical staff on that day.

Baragwanath Hospital is part of the teaching hospital complex of the Medical School of the University of the Witwatersrand. As such, members of the staff enjoy the privileges of members of the clinical teaching staff and junior members are involved in the training scheme for Registrars. High standards are thus mandatory as befits a teaching hospital. But it remains inadequate in terms of the population it is supposed to serve.

Township Administration

Throughout the 1950's and 60's the administration of Soweto was in the hands of the Johannesburg City Council, under its Non-European Affairs Department (NEAD) which was directly in charge of the locations. The NEAD liaised with the residents through municipal offices located in each location and through sponsored and selected Africans forming the Advisory Boards.

When the Nationalist Party took power in 1948 it clamoured to take over complete control of the running of Soweto to destroy any semblance of a united African voice in urban areas. In 1961 it passed the Urban Bantu Council Act which demanded the establishment of ethnic or linguistic councils instead of advisory boards in urban areas. The object of the system was "the integration of the urban Bantu into the systems of government of their homelands and the extension thereof." It goes without saying the UBC became a dismal failure in the location. After the 1976 events it emerged that the UBC's new nickname was "Useless Boys' Club," a reference not only to its failure but also to its members, who by working with the system deserved the white man's epithet—boy.

The apartheid regime was not to be deterred by the failure of the UBC and in 1972 a proclamation in a government gazette terminated the administration of urban areas by local municipal council. Instead the ruling of Soweto was taken over in July 1973 by the Bantu Affairs Administration Boards (BAAB), a specially created government machine. Soweto and other townships are thus under direct state control—a state which is unrepresentative of members of the community it governs!

The lives of more than one million Sowetonians fall under the West Rand Bantu Affairs Administration Board, known as WRAB, whose boss is Manie Mulder, brother of a South African cabinet minister.

Already after its first year of existence the board proposed to increase Soweto house rentals by R2 a month. As in other low paid communities where alternative housing does not exist, rents are of important concern to Soweto residents.

51

From the years of the founding of Soweto to the late 1950's rent payment was charged according to wage earnings and incomes of tenants. For instance white-collar workers, the professionals and businessmen paid more rent than the low-paid unskilled labourers, the disabled and pensioners. The municipality issued assessment forms to the tenants annually to determine the rent according to wages earned. The rents varied from R1·50 to R2·60 a month according to the number of rooms.

Rent defaulters were punished by being evicted from the houses and their possessions, like furniture, confiscated and sold by the council to recover the "debts." Today the residents are paying from R8 to R10 a month with an additional electricity bill where applicable. Rent is paid at local municipal offices staffed by clerks, cashiers and the policemen nicknamed "the blackjacks." It is the blackjacks who carry out raids at dawn on rent-defaulters with subpoenas to appear in court. Failure to pay rent means prosecution in court, serving a prison sentence, having property confiscated and sold by the municipality and losing the right to rent a house. Should the "culprit" lose his job after serving sentence he is "repatriated" to a Bantustan.

In the 1960's, a man named Mr. P. W. J. Carr was the manager of the Non-European Affairs Department when stringent measures to ensure rent payment were introduced after the Soweto residents had been accused of owing the council millions of rands. "Mr. Oppenheimer wants his millions back," Mr. Carr used to say when admonishing Soweto dwellers.

The original loan for the development of Soweto had been provided for the Johannesburg City Council by the Anglo American Corporation whose chairman is Mr. Harry Oppenheimer.

Other income for the WRAB/BAAB comes from profits obtained from "booze" sold to the inhabitants. At present 80% of profits of "white" liquor other than "Bantu" beer sold by the board goes to the Government to subsidise "development" of the Bantustans. In the fiscal year ending April 1975, the board gave the government R1,239,090 from this source and retained only R309,770. Another source of income to the board is the profit made on Bantu beer—tamele— which was expected to amount to R4·4 million at the end of the 1975 fiscal year. Beer profits are also used to subsidise rents and even the inadequate sporting facilities.

It is estimated that Sowetonians drink R17 million a year, thus through boozing they are compelled to finance their existence as "cheap labour tools" of the South African economy.

Yet another source of revenue is the levy which employers of Black labour pay to the board—a composite fee of R1·50 a month on each worker except domestic servants whose employers pay 50c a month.

Rents, liquor and the labour levy are the sole sources of revenue for the BAAB's. General taxation does not subsidise the development of facilities in the neglected townships.

Sport and Culture

There is only one "national" stadium where games are played in Soweto. The national games including soccer and regional school sporting events are by Soweto standards rated as "national." It is the Orlando Stadium, whose maximum seating and standing capacity is 15,000. When big games are played—boxing is also popular—30,000 sports fans are jam-packed into the Stadium. Scattered here and there are a few smaller football pitches, nine small community halls and a number of delapidated children's playgrounds. There are two swimming pools, one cinema, an amphitheatre, an undeveloped park, and derelict golf course where golfers are allowed membership provided they produce a valid pass-book to the WRAB officials. The former Transvaal Non-European Golf Union was ordered to disband by WRAB who took over control of the golf course.

Sowetonians are denied proper sporting and recreational facilities because, according to apartheid policy, blacks in urban areas are only there for the sole purpose of serving the white man and not to idle around.

Sowetonians have an abundance of churches. There are 175 church buildings and 900 sects, quite a big number because the churches too are divided into tribal groupings. The apartheid regime does not only believe in God the Father, Son and Holy Ghost, it also believes in God of the Vaderland, the English, the Zulus, the Xhosas, the Vendas and so on. Even if a Sowetonian is an irregular and non-paying churchgoer, his wedding, baptism of his babies and funeral must be blessed by a priest! The day a Sowetonian wants any of these rites performed he meets his church dues somehow. Because of racial discrimination and the fake policy of Africanisation of the churches, the established churches like the Lutheran, Anglican, Roman Catholic, Presbyterian and others are losing out and failing to attract new members. Sowetonians as workers reserve Sunday as a day to do household chores like washing and cleaning, visiting the sick and attending weddings and funerals. Today, if a Sowetonian priest wants to eat he must conduct more weddings and burial service. At such services the Sowetonians willingly contribute to the family of God.

The Zenzele Young Women's Christian Association is the only women's organisation with its own cultural centre in Soweto. Even so, the building of the centre was only allowed by the authorities who at the time wanted to successfully hoodwink the aspiring African middle class into moving to Dube Township from Sophiatown. When in later years the members of the Young Women's Christian Association wanted to extend the centre, the government refused. The government reminded the YWCA that according to the policy of separate development Africans will only be allowed development in their own homelands and not in urban areas. The government changed face again early in 1973 and allowed the extension of the centre because of international pressure mounting against the YWCA South African affiliates who were accused of racial segregation.

The International YWCA movement was considering kicking out the South African affiliates.

Other international women's organisations like the National Council of Women, Housewives League and the Association of Professional and Businesswomen have branches in Soweto. What is ludicrous is that when the National Council of African Women wanted to build creches and nursery schools in Soweto the government told them to do so in the homelands. And like an obedient baby the National Council of African Women looked for homeland welfare projects. Of course it met with dismal failure because working as a united group of African mothers how could its projects be divided into ethnic groupings? The Housewives League always organise expensive dances to raise funds for "scholarships". They are still to show the world a successful product of their project. The Association for Professional and Businesswomen is fond of organising meetings for its "class." These meetings turn out to be fashion parades and tea parties. Amidst poverty and exploitation the Soweto affiliates of these bourgeois organisations are engaged in futile copycat projects which are foreign to a working class community.

What Soweto women need are organisations which will rally the women on bread and butter issues. Against the passes, making demands for more wages and better working conditions, demands for improved education for their children, demands for cheaper improved transport facilities, demands for the right to lead normal family lives.

Working on the *Mail*

Nkosinathi was only three weeks old when I returned to work because I had withdrawn all the meagre maternity allowance. My mother was still working as a dressmaker and she agreed to look after my baby, thus Nkosinathi was saved the agony of being shunted from house to house in search of grannies. By 1966, I earned more than R10 a week, thus liable to the Pay-as-you-earn Tax Scheme and Maternity Benefit Fund. I must point out that strictly speaking this form of taxation in South Africa was specifically designed for the white privileged class whose wages are never less than R10 a week. In addition to this tax, the Bantustan levy was deducted from my salary. Only a fraction of the African professional or skilled labourers earn money that qualifies them for the PAYE Scheme. The majority of African women hardly earn R6 a week.

After working for a few weeks back with the *World*, I walked out because I could no longer tolerate reporting sensational crime stories. I had, after all, gained typing experience and learnt how to present news.

I walked to the *Rand Daily Mail* offices and asked if I could get a job as a reporter. I remember the "Township" News Editor of the *Mail* saying to me that the *Mail* had never employed a black woman before. I argued and persuaded him. He gave in by saying I could give it a try as a freelancer. The *Mail* had a big African readership. It was a liberal newspaper which had recently published a series of stories exposing the horrifying conditions of South African prisons.

I started as a freelance reporter but at the same time I was pressing to be employed on a full-time basis, the reasons being, first, all African part-time journalists were refused registration as full-time workers by the labour office. This meant they were employed on a daily labourer's permit, whose fee was R1·50 a month and renewable at the end of each month. This meant that each reporter had to make the usual nerve-racking call at the pass office once a month. Secondly, working as a freelancer meant hard work in order to earn a living wage. Payment was according to the number of stories published by the newspapers you freelanced for. In order to keep good reporters for itself, the *Mail* offered a basic retainer's fee which was not adequate by any standards and a part-timer lost should he not be productive enough. To overcome the labour registration hazard, I did not take a discharge from the *World*, I now and again popped in there with sensational crime stories.

To the *Mail* I brought in the right type of stories—like the mass removal of Africans from their own areas, because of the Group Areas Act. Stories of political trials, of strikes by African workers and so on. By this time the *Mail* needed African reporters because white journalists need special permits to enter African areas. Although an African needed a permit to enter other African areas it was invariably easier to sneak in if you were African. I enjoyed the art of sneaking in and was able to get good stories for the *Mail*. This was the time of the notorious "resettlement" areas—Limehill, Stinkwater and other removal areas. I remember in Limehill about five babies died in my arms—at different times—because of exposure or malnutrition, because their parents had been forcibly dumped in the open veld without any food and shelter. Together with Father Cosmas Desmond and others, we laid a tombstone in one such grave to commemorate such an agonising death.

The tears of those bereaved mothers still haunt my mind today. After making my name, the *Rand Daily Mail* had no choice but to think of employing me on a full-time basis. They were reluctant at first because the whole South African Associated Newspapers Group had never employed an African woman before. The Group had to consider what salary to pay me. Not forgetting the toilet facilities in a country where people of different racial groups cannot even share a toilet. I remember that one day I was so pressed I had to go to the loo. At this stage SAAN had not yet allocated a toilet for me, so I went to the Ladies. While I was sitting there a group of angry white women came and pulled me out of the seat. SAAN had no way of defending itself because the law required that there should be separate toilets for each racial group. Subsequently I was given a whole block of toilets on the ground floor. It was a bonanza!

Another physical assault on me as a black person happened hundreds of miles from Johannesburg. It was at a restaurant in Lichtenburg, in the Northern

Transvaal. I had been travelling in a car with a group of African women who had been to a three-day annual meeting of the National Council of African Women. I was at the conference for press coverage. As we were driving on this hot Sunday afternoon, we all became thirsty and decided to stop the car after spotting a restaurant.

I then walked over to buy cold drinks for the whole group. On approaching the restaurant, the outside of the door did not display the customary segregated entrance sign. I went in straight to the counter and ordered five bottles of Coke and Fanta. There were no customers standing at the counter at the time. From the face of the woman shop attendant I read an expression of mute consternation. It puzzled me. Without saying a word, the man in attendance with her picked up an empty bottle of coca-cola and came out from the counter towards the huge freezer standing next to me. I thought he was going to take out the drinks I had ordered. The next thing I felt was a thud on my head. I fell on the ground and fainted. I regained consciousness later, as cold water was being poured on me. I was lying on the pavement. In my stupor, I could hear women's voices saying "She is alright now." They picked me up and helped me to my feet heading to the car. I gradually recalled what had happened. I got very angry. In the car the women explained to me that as they were sitting in the car, they saw two men coming out of the restaurant carrying what looked like a woman's body by its legs and arms. The men dumped the body on the pavement outside the shop and returned inside. Recognising the colour of the body's dress, they were sure it was me. In panic they all ran out of the car to find out what had happened. A "deranged" white man came out of the restaurant, shouting that "no kaffir had ever entered his shop through the front door". Local Africans, who had by now gathered around, had pointed to a side window through which blacks purchased food from that restaurant. But then we Jo'burg Africans were used to using the same doors in certain City restaurants which do not display segregated entrance signs.

I, in turn, related the attack to the group, and we decided to drive to the local police station. As we approached it a car overtook us at full speed, stopped and a white man brandishing a gun got out and threatened to shoot us if we drove to the police station.

We decided that reporting to the police was not worth risking our lives. I would instead report the assault in Johannesburg. That rascal's car followed us a few miles out of Lichtenburg.

We arrived in Johannesburg after midnight. We were all tired and I decided I would discuss the attack first at the *Mail* before going to the police. On the following day, the *Mail* News Editor advised me to go straight to John Vorster Square and lay a charge of assault. He explained that should the *Mail* publish the case, the police, government and its supporters would accuse it of being sensational and harming race relations. The *Mail* would instead give full coverage of the case once it was in court. The News Editor asked a crime reporter to

56

accompany me to John Vorster Square. In the SAAN car, driven by an African, I sat in front, the other reporter at the back.

On arrival at John Vorster Square the crime reporter and I used separate entrances leading to the "Nie-Blankes"—"Non-White"—charge office. Inside a mid-high wall partition separated whites from blacks. So my colleague spoke to the man of his colour, while I told the African one that I was accompanied by a colleague who was explaining my case at the other side. The "colleague" reference puzzled the African police who asked if "that white man" was not my boss.

Then the policeman from the other side came and instructed the African one to take my statement. He stood by as I described the attack. Before I started my colleague asked to be excused. Calling each other's first names we said bye bye to each other. It was all foreign to both policemen. After dictating the details to the African police, the white one asked for the name of the restaurant. I did not know it, but said I could point it out on the spot. He then asked for the description of my attacker. I told him, adding that it would not be difficult to identify him since at the time of the attack there was only the woman and the man in the shop. The man had also said he was the owner of the restaurant. I gave the names of my witnesses. They were all respectable women, teachers and nurses. One of them had actually grown up in Lichtenburg and was now wife of a lawyer. She was also the national president of the National Council of African Women. The white police took the statement and said I would be contacted when the investigation was finished.

After a long lapse, I went back to John Vorster Square to inquire about what had happened to the investigation. A few days after my inquiry I received a note from the investigating officer stating that after a thorough investigation, it was decided there was not enough evidence to institute prosecution. That was the end of the case. By this time the *Mail* had no legal power to publish the attack. It had been through the hands of the police.

Being on the road collecting good stories which exposed the brutality of the apartheid system had its dangers. One day, photographer Peter Magubane and I were stopped by the Security Police as we were driving around in Limehill. We were thoroughly searched on the spot. The police demanded our press cards which we did not possess anyway. In South Africa it is the police who issue press cards! We produced the passbooks which they demanded. Peter's film spool and my notebook were confiscated. The police then led us out of Limehill and warned us we would be arrested on return.

Because the *Mail* was taking a long time in deciding on my job prospects I staged a demonstration by walking out and taking a full-time job with *Post* and *Drum*.

I went back to the *World* to get a discharge. The white accountant wanted to backdate the discharge to the day I walked out of the newspaper. I defended myself by saying "But really I've been still working for you." It was true. For the two years of freelance work I did send crime stories for the *World* publication. I got an updated discharge, thus escaping the question "What have you been doing in the past two years" from the labour office. In South Africa's white cities, Africans get "repatriated" to the homelands if it is deemed they had been idling for a period.

As I was now in great demand, I wanted to prove a point to the *Mail* that as an intelligent black woman journalist I was a force to be reckoned with. After only three months with *Post* and *Drum*, the *Rand Daily Mail* wrote a letter offering me a permanent job. I went back. I rejoined the *Mail* because the *Post* newspaper, which was a weekly, was not as outspoken as the *Mail*. It also depended a lot on crime sensation stories and pin-up girls picture. *Drum* magazine was running a few pages quarterly. During its heyday, *Drum* was popular for its coverage of feature stories which involved political organisations. I had been unfortunate in that I had entered the journalistic trade at a time when outstanding black and white journalists were either in gaol or in exile, banned or underground.

The publishing houses were being seriously threatened by tougher legislation of press censorship. The remnants of press freedom was in the process of being further curtailed. Given the prevailing conditions I was relieved to have been called back by the *Mail*. It was a good personal achievement. If I remember correctly this happened towards the beginning of 1968. My work on the *Mail* was however destined to be short-lived.

Not long after I returned I experienced one of the happiest moments of my life. I became secretly engaged to Kenneth Rankin, a Scottish doctor, whom I had met during one of my "daring" assignments. Because our respective complexions are similar to the advertisement for the Scotch whisky "Black and White" we could not get engaged in public in that sorry country. Ours was an illegal affair.

Our courting was a risky business. I recall an attack on us as we were driving down Jan Smuts Avenue one night. I had made the mistake of sitting in the front seat as Kenneth was driving. The car behind us suddenly pulled next to ours on my side as we stopped at the red lights. We heard voices screaming and we looked. There were six bully-like white fellows in the other car, gesticulating with their fists and shouting at us, pointing at me in particular. The lights changed, and Kenneth drove off at full speed. The other car followed suit. It was a chase. Thrice it drove ahead of us and tried to block us but Kenneth managed to steer clear. He made a mistake leaving the motorway and turning into a smaller road. All the six men jumped out of the car, one held a gun and was threatening to use it. We had locked our doors. The men surrounded the car attempting to open the doors. I braved it, and unlocked mine, the next moment I was dragged out and shaken by the men as if they were loosening dust stuck in a blanket. They hurled me back into the car, but in the back seat. All insults which belong to the gutter were flung at me. I was warned by the men that "in future I should know where my place is." They got back into their car and drove off. We followed at slow speed and made a detour at the first chance we got. We did not drive to our planned destination, but Kenneth dropped me off at a taxi rank instead.

A few days later, Kenneth left the country, after we had planned that I would follow him with Nkosinathi by whatever means. A few weeks later I was, instead, an inmate of a solitary confinement cell held under the South African Terrorism Act. Suddenly my life was in complete ruins, with the shadow of death lurking in the surrounds of Pretoria Central Prison.

Detention

I was detained on May 12, 1969 at about 2 a.m. We heard knocking and woke to the flashing of torches outside and shouts of "Police! Police! Open the door!" We all got up—my mother, myself and my two brothers—and the police came in. There were three white policemen, one white policewoman and an African policeman, all in plain clothes.

They demanded Joyce Sikakane and I said it was myself and they produced a warrant of arrest under Section 6 of the Terrorism Act. They said they wanted to search the house. They were all brandishing their guns about and so they searched the house and took away whatever documents and personal papers—all my letters for example—they wished. The policewoman was guarding me the whole time.

After about two hours they told me to get dressed, as I was still in my nightie; I did so and was escorted to the car. I was afraid to wake Nkosinathi who was still sleeping, so I left him without saying goodbye.

On the way out of Soweto the car dropped off the African policeman in Meadowlands. I remember him saying "Thank you my baas, you caught the terrorist. I hope you get the information you want out of her."

We drove off to John Vorster Square (Security Police HQ) where another policeman got out, and then on again. When I asked where we were going, the only reply was that I was being detained under the Terrorism Act. I was terrified: I didn't see myself as a terrorist and didn't know why I should be detained under the Terrorism Act.

I was taken to Pretoria Central prison. They knocked on the big door, the guard looked out and then opened the gate and I was led in. First we went to the office; they spoke to the matron and papers were signed. My engagement ring was taken from me—I was upset about that. Then we crossed the prison yard to another part of the prison. In the yard were about a hundred African women, some with babies on their backs, some sitting on the ground, some with vegetable baskets full of onions, pumpkins and so on, whom I could see were vendors who had been arrested for illegally selling vegetables in the street. As I came into the yard, the policeman shouted to the women to shut their eyes.

This was because I was a Terrorism Act detainee, to be held incommunicado, which meant no-one should know who or where I was. I was taken past and up some stairs, where the two policemen escorting me greeted another man as Colonel Okamp.

He told the matron to take me to a cell. And I heard her ask "Is she a condemned woman?" as I was shown into a cell with a bright blinding light that made me see sparks.

Okamp immediately said "No, no, not that one, I made a mistake." So I was taken out and led along to the common shower room, where there were lots of women prisoners, some naked under the showers, some undressing, some waiting their turn. The matron told me to undress, which I did, and got under the cold shower. I could tell the other women knew there was something special about me, being under escort and alone and jumping the queue like that.

After the cold shower I picked up my paper bag of clothes—the matron told me not to dress—and I was led to a cell. It was narrow and high, situated in what I later discovered was the isolation wing. The outer steel door was opened and then the inner barred door; I went in and the matron locked first one and then the other.

So there I was, in this tall narrow empty cell, gazing around. There was a small high hole covered with mesh, for ventilation. And it was very cold: May is the beginning of winter in South Africa and we had already had some frost. Suddenly I heard women's voices coming from outside in the yard, talking. I was horrified to hear them talking about their love affairs inside prison—the experienced women telling the freshers what to expect, how some were chosen as husbands and some as wives, and generally describing the whole scene to them. It gave me a real fright, standing there naked. I at once got my paper bag and put my panties on!

When I looked around at the contents of the cell all I saw was a damp sisal mat, rolled up, and three grey blankets, also damp and smelling of urine. That was all. I just sat down on the mat and waited.

It wasn't until 7 o'clock that evening that the cell door opened. There was a white wardress and an African woman prisoner in prison uniform, who shoved a plate of food through the door, along the floor, together with a galvanised bucket. All the time the wardress stood between me and the prisoner, so I should not be seen. Then they left, locking the doors behind them. But I heard them open the next cell and then I knew I wasn't alone: if the next cell was occupied I wasn't the only woman detainee.

From then on the pattern of prison life was always the same. In the morning at about 7 a.m. the cell door was opened, the shit bucket and empty plate taken out and a plate of porridge and cup of coffee put in. There was a bucket of sometimes warm water too, to wash oneself and one's underclothes. Lunch was usually about noon, though it could be earlier—on Sundays it was about 10.30—and consisted of izinkobe or dry mealies—corn kernels—which had been boiled but were still dry and hard. There was a beverage too, some sort of drink, which the prisoners used to call puza'mandla—drink power! Then at about 2 p.m. came supper, which was soft maize porridge with one or two pieces of meat, possibly pork, in it. That was all until the next day.

For the first few days I didn't eat anything. I was frightened, angry, depressed, wondering why I had been detained, scared of what might happen, and crying most of the time. By the third day, I had cried all my tears out. At least, I think it was the third day. Two huge policemen, with layers and layers of chin, came for me. I asked where they were taking me and they said, to give an account of your sins.

I was driven in a big Cadillac, with a policeman on either side of me and two more in front. We went to the Compol building (police HQ) in Pretoria. Knock, knock again, the police escort identify themselves and we drive in.

Down some corridors to an office. It looks like any other office except it has these wooden partitions. Right facing me is a stone sink and then there's a desk and a few chairs. I can see it's a work room. All along the walls is this wooden partitioning, covering the windows but capable of being drawn back. It kind of encloses the room, insulates it from outside. And just off this room is a sort of gym closet with punch bags—and a huge African policeman with fierce red eyes standing there. While I was being interrogated policemen kept trooping in to practice boxing on the punch bags.

Interrogation

There was a constant stream of policemen, about fifteen or twenty, coming into the room, as if they were going on stage. They were brandishing guns, holding documents, smoking cigarettes, greeting me, some scowling at me. They all looked different, some like bulldogs, some like Alsatians, some like timid cats. Some of them behaved with great politeness, like perfect gentlemen. I think this performance was just put on to confuse me, for the next thing was Major Swanepoel coming in. He is the most sadistic and most feared of all the police interrogators; several people have died as a result of his "questioning."

"Have you heard of Major Swanepoel?" he said. "I am Major Swanepoel." All the other policemen gave way to him, treating him very deferentially. Then interrogation began.

They fired questions and statements at me; all of a sudden they were all talking about me and my personal life—all my experiences, which they seem to know better than I did! As they did so they incidentally revealed the extent of their informer network: I found they knew about all sorts of incidents in my career—the story about the Malawian air hostesses being allowed to stay in an all-white hotel, for instance, that I had been working on when I was detained. I also discovered, from things they said, who else had been questioned: Winnie

61

Mandela, wife of ANC leader Nelson Mandela, and Rita Ndzanga, for instance. They had interrogated many other people I knew, and from what they knew I could see they had been tortured to extract the information.

From me they wanted confirmation: that certain things had been done, that I had knowingly participated, and whatever else I could add. From what they know one has to judge what to admit and what to hide and what one might not manage to hide—because it flashes into your mind what risk to others is involved, and also the possibility of being tortured yourself and whether the type of information you have is worth dying for. I knew that in our case what we had been doing was something that would not, in any other country, be considered "terroristic": we were involved with the welfare of political prisoners, helping to make arrangements for families of prisoners to visit their husbands or parents. And so why not admit it? Yes, I did that—so what? We hadn't been involved in anything connected with violence or arms—that would have called for other methods of interrogation. As far as I was concerned they were more interested in getting information about the underground communication network.

The interrogation lasted right through until the following day. They took turns, and took breaks. I was just standing there. I would be tired, I would squat down, I would jump about a bit. I was shown the bricks—the torture bricks on which the men detainees are made to stand. The questioning went on, without food, without anything, till the following morning. Then I was taken back to my cell.

It was about ten days before I was taken again for interrogation. This time it lasted for three whole days because this time they were concerned with taking a statement. Under the Terrorism Act a detainee may be held until a statement to the satisfaction of the Commissioner of Police has been given, and the purpose of the interrogation is to obtain such a statement which can then be used against you or someone else. They still ask questions: anything you admit goes down on the statement.

This time my interrogation took place on the third floor of Compol building, and the interrogators were Major Botha and Major Coetzee. They were trained and experienced political officers. Oh, they were courteous gentlemen, but I could sense hatred—they hated every bit of me. But they had to get what they wanted from me.

They put the proposal that I should be a state witness, giving evidence for the state against the others. I asked why should I do that? and they said, well, you're young, you're an intelligent girl, you have a fiancé outside the country. If you are afraid to give evidence because of what your organisation will do to you, we can always give you another name and find a job in one of our embassies abroad—say in Malawi or London, where you can join your fiancé!

All the time, because of what they wanted out of me, they were at pains to explain that they were not against Africans or black people in general. They were only against communists. They argued that people like myself, young, intelligent, pretty, etc., were being misled by communists. They, on the other hand, were offering me a chance. I found this insulting. How could they sit there, admit that apartheid was a repressive system, which they did while maintaining that racism occurred all over the world. What hypocrites I said inside me to say communists had misled me into wanting to change the system. I didn't need any communists to tell me apartheid is evil. I know. Nor would I join the enemy camp for the sake of self preservation.

So I told Major Botha and Major Coetzee I was not interested in their offer. They said in that case you are going to be here a long time. Others had given evidence, they said. If you refuse we have lots of other evidence we can use, the others are willing.

In the end they took a statement. Under the law it's supposed to be made of one's own volition—but I wondered how, under the circumstances of indefinite detention under the Terrorism Act, anything can be called of one's own volition. I came to the point when I agreed to some of the things they said—well, if you say that, yes, it's so.

After they had taken the statement Major Coetzee said "Well, Joyce, we think you should think seriously about our offer. We will transfer you to another prison, so you can think over the offer." Then they repeated their offer of a job in London. I didn't bother to reply yes or no, I just kept silent. And I was taken back to my cell.

In Nylstroom Prison

About a week later I was transferred to Nylstroom prison. I didn't know the exact date, not having a watch or calendar. Being taken to Nylstroom had some irony, in that one of my "offences," one of the things I had done which led to my being detained, was that at one time I had been part of a group of women who had been to visit prisoners at Nylstroom. It is a women's prison in the Transvaal, north of Johannesburg, and there were political prisoners there from the Cape, who had not heard from or about their families for years. A letter enquiring about their families had been smuggled out by one woman and when it reached us we decided to go as a group to visit the women in Nylstroom. And now I was going to be an inmate of Nylstroom Prison.

In Nylstroom, although still a detainee, I was given a bed with a mattress. There can be proper facilities if they wish it. The bed was part of the better conditions promised me if I would consider giving evidence, and in fact the sheets were even starched. You can imagine how I felt sleeping in starched sheets! I itched all over. The food was the same, just a few spoonfuls more perhaps. But the cell was bigger than at Pretoria, and a different shape. This one was squarer, wider with a lower ceiling, unlike the high narrow Pretoria one. And there was a window through which I could see out and altogether there wasn't the terrible confined and depressed feeling as in Pretoria. And there was a table and a chair!

The matron used to bring me books to read, all crime stories and thrillers which gave me terrible nightmares. One day I complained that I couldn't read the books, so she brought another collection, amongst which was one by (I think) J. M. Miller, an author who wrote about the Resistance movement against the Nazis in Europe, and this book was about the escape route over the Pyrenees, and how the Resistance functioned. I had my suspicions that the book had been put there to encourage me to try to escape—only to be found hanging from a window, or perhaps shot—but anyway it certainly boosted my spirit of resistance too. I did not intend to risk an escape bid, nor to commit suicide—although there were many times, particularly at night, when I was so lonely and depressed I felt anything would be better than this. I had a game to play at such times, a "blindman" game when I shut my eyes and pretended I was blind—not able to see the walls, the bars and the rest.

At Nylstroom, instead of proper exercise, the matron used to take me to an isolated yard where I could sit or jump around—all alone. I just used to sit there for about 30 minutes. I was so depressed, I didn't feel like jumping around. I felt I had no strength. So I just used to sit or lie on the ground, watching the red ants going in and out of their holes. I watched them carrying their food and corpses of dead insects, and I used to count them. It was a beautiful game, counting ants. I had been too long in solitary confinement.

Every so often, the Special Branch officers used to come and ask "Have you thought it over? Will you agree?" and I used to answer "When are you releasing me? When are you charging me? I want to go back home." About every ten to fourteen days they came and said the same thing. I replied as I did before. It was after a long, long time when on the last of these calls, they came and said "Well, we have come to take you."

I said, "Where are you taking me?" "We are taking you home."

Of course I was taken back to Pretoria Central, to the same cell I had occupied before. But there was one remarkable change: on the wall was now written the name Shanthie Naidoo. Shanthie was my friend and now I knew she had been detained too.

That same afternoon the cells were opened, first mine, and then four others, and we were taken out. I'll never forget the feelings of that moment, a kind of muted consternation, when we five women all saw each other. There was Winnie Mandela, Rita Ndzanga, Martha Dhlamini, Thokozile Mngoma—and of course we each half expected, as our interrogators had said, that the others had agreed to give evidence. But they hadn't. I remember we hugged each other hard: it was too good to be true. We felt this was a moment of victory and we were together. Shanthie was not there: they were playing the same game with her as they had with me, trying to make her agree to give evidence against us.

We were then led to the office where security police were waiting, and there was no doubt about their hostility. We were, they said, to appear in court tomorrow, and we would be charged (though we were not told what the charges were). Then we were taken back to the cells. We asked to be allowed to stay together but this was refused, and we did not see each other again until we were taken to court. But that night we were singing freedom songs—singing our lungs out, each in our separate cell.

The next day we were taken to court, where we met the men who were being charged with us. Again there was this muted feeling of consternation: what the police had said and what we now realised was true. Now it was a question of seeing how everyone was, who had sold out and who was still battling. There were some of the people who weren't there; we guessed from this that they had agreed to give evidence, but because of what we had been through we didn't feel like saying anything against them. It was just too bad—bad luck.

In court there was real jubilation—hugs and kisses and clenched fists. Our relatives were also there in the public gallery when we came into court, and we learned that they had instructed a lawyer to defend us. We were charged under the Suppression of Communism Act. It was 1 December—seven months since I had been arrested. There were 22 of us altogether, five women and 17 men. Among them Lawrence and Rita Ndzanga, both trade unionists. During the 1960's Lawrence was national secretary of the Railway and Harbour Workers Union, and until its banning an executive member of the South African Congress of Trade Unions (SACTU). Rita was secretary of the Toy Workers Union. The apartheid regime embarked on the full-scale repression of the progressive labour movement and in 1963 both Lawrence and Rita were banned, which means being subject to restriction orders, not allowed to continue working or travel outside one's home district. Both had been detained at the same time as myself, and brutally assaulted by the security police. Another of the accused was Peter Magubane, my news photographer colleague with the *Rand Daily Mail*.

On Trial

We were charged on 21 main charges, most of them concerned with membership of the African National Congress, which had been officially banned in 1961. Some of the charges alleged plotting to obtain explosives and commit sabotage and other serious things, but mostly they alleged various activities on behalf of the ANC. We were all charged together, all incriminated with each other.

The first day was taken up with arranging about the defence lawyers, and with our parents and of course with finding out what had happened to each other, when and why each of us was interrogated and so on. Interrogation had taught us the enemy's workings and intentions—they wanted us to quarrel amongst ourselves, to be divided and, above all, to be bitter against each other. So we decided that this was something we just had to face; whatever information they had extracted from us was too bad and whatever they didn't manage to get from us—well and good. Some of the men had been tortured with electric shocks, and amongst the women Rita Ndzanga had been assaulted.

Rita had been a trade unionist, and of course trade union organisers are hated by the police. Toko Mngoma had been in the executive of the ANC Women's League and Martha Dhlamini was also an old ANC campaigner. Winnie Mandela was Nelson's wife and involved in past protest campaigns. In fact all the women had a history of political activity except me, so the police were only too happy to settle accounts and prosecute them. And amongst the younger people on trial including myself, our attempts to do something about apartheid repression were considered great audacity. As far as the state was concerned we too had a lot to answer for. There were several older men amongst us, such as one about 70 years old, who had been an active ANC member in Alexandra Township in the old days and who was tortured during interrogation. Lawrence Ndzanga was a trade unionist, and Elliot Shabangu had been an ANC organiser, so the police had something to settle with them as well.

Then the trial began, as usual with political trials in South Africa, with witnesses whose testimony can be shown to incriminate some or all of the accused. Often this testimony is very wide and is the sort of thing that wouldn't be considered incriminating anywhere else, only in South Africa.

At the time, the government was preparing for elections and wanted to use our trial for advertising purposes, to show that it was still very powerful and in control, that it had caught these communists and put them on trial. That was the political purpose behind our trial.

The first witnesses were some white people who had been in some kind of contact with the accused, and who gave evidence for the state and exposed the involuntary nature of it. Some had been tortured, some threatened and anyway, being detained under the Terrorism Act, how can they be said to have made a statement of their own volition, knowing that they would not be released until they did so? Other witnesses appeared, who said the same thing—their evidence was worthless. And even if it had been made voluntarily, it was nothing that proved any kind of terrorist conspiracy. There was nothing really there against us.

Shanthie Naidoo and Nomwe Mamkhala were brought into the witness box and refused to give evidence. This was after we had been told in court that Shanthie wanted to give evidence, and the prosecutor asked us if we were going to forgive her! Shanthie herself was brought from jail without being told where she was being taken. Suddenly she found herself in the witness box. She said she had been interrogated continuously for five days, during which she had not been allowed to sleep, rest or sit down. She had been threatened that her whole family would be arrested if she refused to speak. In court she said she would not give evidence against us because two of us were her friends—myself and Winnie Mandela. When asked by the judge for her reasons for refusing to give evidence,

Shanthie answered "I will not be able to live with my conscience if I do." For refusing, she and Nomwe were sentenced to two months imprisonment. They were not released from detention however. They went back to jail and were given prison clothes but none of the other prisoners' rights such as visits or letters etc. The security police can thus override the law and keep convicted prisoners incommunicado. At the end of the two months, the prison clothes were removed and ordinary clothes—the same ones they had brought with them when first detained—were returned. After that Shanthie spent four more months in solitary as a detainee under the Terrorism Act. We did not hear about Nomwe Mamkhala's fate.

As it turned out, the trial rebounded on the government, because instead of the evidence being to the liking of the state, it exposed the state's methods of getting evidence and demonstrated the bravery and resistance of the men and women on trial. There was good coverage in the white press and also internationally, and there was an observer from the International Commission of Jurists. The quality of the evidence made fools of the Special Branch and their accusations, it made fools of the whole Terrorism Act and all the conspiracy laws of South Africa because, as our lawyer pointed out, some of the acts alleged had taken place when one of the accused was still a toddler, so how could he be held responsible by association?

And because the evidence was so ridiculous and the publicity so bad, the state decided to abandon the case, to withdraw the charges. This was 16 February 1970. We could not believe it when we heard the judge say "You are acquitted!" We began to leave the court in single file, between two rows of police, to go and meet our relatives, who were already singing and celebrating. The police refused to let us out and instead took us to a room, where Captain Dekker announced that he was detaining us again. There was a great protest: I remember shouting and I threw a fist at him, but I'm not sure if it landed. The police confiscated everything we had, including all our legal documents, and we were whisked off under guard, back to Pretoria Central.

It all happened so quickly that we hadn't had time to get used to the idea of being free. Nor had we really believed in the acquittal—it just couldn't be true. In any case we had been told so many times during interrogation that we were going to spend 15 years in jail if we were lucky, more if we were not, and we had come to accept imprisonment. So we weren't so surprised to be taken back to detention.

But it was just as bad. I went back to the same cell, and there I stayed for the next four months.

This time there was no exercise, or only very occasionally. There were constant battles between us and the matron and the other officers because we kept demanding to be released, as the court had released us. A magistrate came fortnightly to hear our complaints, as a matter of routine, and we demanded to know why we were detained since we had already been tried and acquitted. We complained about conditions in the cells and demanded to be allowed various

67

things. It all fell on deaf ears; the magistrate thought it was all our fault: "Why did you bring yourself here?" he would ask.

Nothing was improved: they didn't clean our cells, or give us cloths and polish so we could clean them ourselves. The food was just the same, and we could spend a week inside without any exercise, just the door opening three times a day to bring in the food and take out the shit bucket. We used to call these buckets SB's—the same name as we gave the Special Branch.

All the loneliness, emptiness and isolation came back, and so did the need to play games. But this time there were no ants to count.

Sometimes at night we would hear screams and the clatter of SB's on the concrete floors—the noise of prisoners fighting in their cells. Then there would be silence, followed by dogs barking, then men's voices and running footsteps towards where the screams had come from. And the next thing we would hear was the sound of real screams, screams of terror, screams of women being sjamboked. Then the screams died out, we heard the dogs being taken back and the men's voices, before everything died down to silence again.

Because we had no contact with the other prisoners we never got to know what the fights were about. But more painful than the screams was listening to the cries of the babies, all day and all night. Many women committed to Pretoria Central had small babies, or were pregnant, so throughout the jail there was this terrible forlorn crying, babies crying for their mothers or because they were hungry. It appeared that the women were taken off to work and the babies were just left in the cells, but we couldn't enquire about anything, so we didn't know why things were happening.

Except when condemned prisoners were going to be hanged, then we could hear singing coming from the men's section in the early hours of the morning, long, never-ending hymns. This meant the men knew a hanging was about to take place.

Re-trial

Eventually after four months I was taken out to the charge office and the following day 18 June 1970 we were back in court. Two of the prisoners who had previously been charged were missing, and we were given to understand that they had agreed to give evidence against us. And as we were sitting there in the dock, wondering why there was a delay, we saw coming up from the cells a man chained between two policemen. As he was being unchained, he raised his head, threw his clenched fist in the air—"Amandla!" Then the older people in the dock recognised him as Benjamin Ramotse. He was a trained freedom fighter and had been captured in Botswana and so tortured he didn't know how he survived.

This was the reason for the new trial. We were to be linked with him, according to the state, in an international ANC conspiracy, or whatever. We were thus charged with the offences he was alleged to have committed as well as the original charges, and the indictment had been changed from the Suppression of Communism Act to the Terrorism Act. Our lawyers objected to this.

They insisted on applying for a separation of trials, on the grounds that none of us had been connected with Ramotse. Our position was that if the state wanted to link us with him that was okay by us, we were prepared to stand trial with him. The lawyers insisted on trying the technical application. Ramotse himself felt we were mad—if there was a chance we should take it. If he stood trial he would continue the struggle.

In the end the application was successful: the trials were separated. We found it painful to be separated from Ramotse, for we had felt it an honour to be with him. The next step was to apply for a discharge, on the grounds that we couldn't be tried twice on the same charges. This application also succeeded, and once more we heard the judge say we were free. None of us stood up, we just sat, until we had to be evicted from court. We didn't believe we were really free.

We were released on 14 September. Benjamin Ramotse was sentenced to 15 years, which he is serving on the notorious Robben Island. In his trial he argued that the South African and Rhodesian police had violated international law by kidnapping him in Botswana. He had been kidnapped in June 1968, and taken to Rhodesia, where he was tortured. Then he had been kept in solitary confinement in South Africa from July for two whole years before coming to trial. Again, he had been mercilessly tortured, by Major Swanepoel at Compol building.

As for the rest of us, out of the original 22 people charged, Rita and Lawrence Ndzanga have subsequently suffered most. Late in 1976, while this book was being written, they were both detained again under the Terrorism Act, later to be charged with "attempting to endanger the maintenance of law and order." But before Lawrence could appear in court, he was reported to have "collapsed and died" in police custody. He was the fifteenth person to have died in detention in a year. At his funeral in Soweto in February 1977, he was described as a worker for the betterment of his people, who died in doubtful circumstances. "Some of us have been in detention," said the speaker, "and we know what happens behind those windowless walls."

Rita was offered bail so she could attend the funeral, but owing to the obstructiveness of the authorities, she was not able to obtain it until too late. As this book went to press her own Terrorism Act trial was continuing. The Ndzangas have three teenage children.

Others have been re-detained recently. Samson Ndou is still in detention, having been picked up before the Soweto uprisings in June 1976. Winnic Mandela was interned from July to December and is now serving her fourth house-arrest banning order. Peter Magubane was banned after our trial and

69

only able to return to being a news photographer in 1975. Then after he and others had taken some of the pictures showing what the police were doing to the school students demonstrations in 1976 he too was interned for several months.

Another of the accused, Paulos Mashaba, is now mentally deranged. During the first trial we noticed that he was behaving like someone whose mind had gone wrong, but the case was dismissed and we were re-detained before our defence counsel had an opportunity to apply for his discharge owing to his state of mind. During the second period of detention, his condition must have worsened because he was sent to Weskoppies Mental Hospital. He was eventually released and now, being a man of "lost memory" in Soweto, Paulos gets picked up now and again by the pass law officers, for being a "vagabond" or vagrant. One of the accused, Joseph Zikalala, fled South Africa in 1974. Ten others, including myself, Martha Dhlamini and Thoko Mngoma, were all served with banning orders, which effectively prevented us from carrying on with our jobs and normal activities. One, Douglas Mvemve, who must now be over 80, had three children involved in the liberation struggle. His son was killed by a petrol bomb which exploded in Lusaka in 1974 and one of his daughters was held in detention for over a year from November 1975 to December 1976. His other daughter is in exile.

After the jail ordeal, Shantie Naidoo applied for an exit permit to leave the country and join her sister in Great Britain. She received British entry facilities. The Minister of the Interior issued her with an exit permit on February 1, only after she gave notice of intention to institute proceedings. She could not leave South Africa, however, as the banning orders restricted her to the magisterial district of Johannesburg. This meant that she could not travel to Jan Smuts Airport, which is outside the area, to catch a plane. The Minister of Justice refused, in March 1971, to give her permission to go to the airport.

She then applied to the Transvaal Supreme Court for an order directing the Minister of Justice to permit her to leave, but the application was denied on June 22, 1971. Mr. Justice Ryburgh held that a restrictive notice under the Suppression of Communism Act is equivalent to a court term of imprisonment. The Appeal Court upheld this decision on December 2, 1971.

Meanwhile the exit permit expired. She got a second one, it expired again. It was only on the third exit permit that the Minister of Justice relaxed her restriction order to enable her to travel to Jan Smuts Airport.

Shanthie Naidoo is now in Europe having been persecuted for many years for no offence but her opposition to apartheid, and for coming from a family which for generations had been involved in the struggle against racism and exploitation. Previously Shanthie worked as a clerk for the Congress of Democrats until September 1962 when that organisation was banned, and then for the non-racial South African Congress of Trade Unions until 1964, when she was served with a five-year banning order which on expiry was extended to another five years.

A Banned Person

On return home Soweto had not changed. Its life went at a maddening speed compared to the inertia of 17 months in detention, most of it in solitary confinement.

What did slow down my activity and that of 21 others I had been detained with was that shortly after our unexpected release we were served with banning orders. Moreover the State had lodged an appeal against our acquittal. We were subjected to strict police surveillance. The spectre of a return to internment was forever in one's mind.

As Peter Magubane and I were on the staff of the *Rand Daily Mail*, the banning orders meant we could not continue our work as journalists. The *Mail's* Editor, Raymond Louw, applied to the Chief Magistrate of Johannesburg for a relaxation of the orders to enable us to continue work for the newspaper. As if to demonstrate the power of the almighty the Minister of Justice refused the application and imposed more stringent orders which barred us from all African areas and townships except those where we lived. We were prohibited from newspaper offices, factories, educational institutions and social and political gatherings. We were both ordered to report weekly to the police. The irony of it was that when these stringent orders were issued Peter Magubane was held on a third spell of detention under Section Six of the Terrorism Act. He was released after spending a total of 586 days incommunicado. In the past he had been assaulted and arrested a number of times by the police who objected to the type of photographs he took.

Back in Soweto as one of the thousands of political outlaws I had to adapt my life accordingly. I had to run the gauntlet.

Soon I had to decide whether to leave the country and join Kenneth who was then working in Zambia—"to make me feel his presence nearer home." After his departure in 1969 his British status to enter the country without a visa was withdrawn by the South African government.

Judging from the hostile treatment meted on us by the political police, it was clear to me that even if I had applied for an exit permit I would not get one. Although friends made plans for me to flee the country I felt chances of a successful escape were nil.

It was these considerations which made me write the following letter to Ken dated June 24, 1971, incidentally my birthday, after speaking to him on the telephone:

"darling Ken,

Speaking to you was the greatest birthday gift I could have wished for. You know what you mean to me. What's happening between us now is beyond our control. What's important is to keep on living. We've been forced to alter our plans. It's hurting and humiliating.

I know you're, probably, the one who has been hurt most because you were waiting all the time while I was taking the decision. It's hard, love, but we've got no choice. I must remain in South Africa.

Ken, I do expect you long to have a family of your own. Do not feel you will be betraying me, if you decide on this. I know this sounds callous, but it's a fact which both of us must face, or perhaps decide on sooner or later.

Love, one of my greatest happiness will be on the day when you become a family man, free of all this torture we are both emotionally involved in now. Because of the love I have for you, I would very much like you to lead a normal life. What I love, I want it to be free and alive."

I felt that if I was not able to leave South Africa it was not fair to continue the engagement.

Police reaction to the telephone call mentioned in the letter was as if I had set Johannesburg on fire. As I spoke to Ken, who was in Lusaka and I in Johannesburg, I was sure that the telephone conversation was tapped. I was at a friend's house in a white Johannesburg suburb. After the call I was escorted back to Soweto by three police cars, one in front and two at the back of the car I was in. It was clear a telephone call between two lovers constituted a threat to the security of the South African State.

Looking for jobs in the City is the biggest source of discontent and bitterness among Sowetonians because job segregation is customary and statutory in South Africa.

A worker looking for employment is faced with the grim prospects of having no choice, of low wages, of appalling working conditions and racial discrimination and the fear of being "repatriated" to the Bantustans if he does not find a job.

From the minute a Sowetonian starts looking for a job he is faced with the cruel reality that as an African he is only wanted as a cheap labour tool by the white economy. And as a proscribed person my labour was not even desirable. So it seemed as a folly that everyday I paged through the job adverts of the national dailies and weeklies knowing full well that domestic work featured mainly for the Africans and the type of work—typing, filing and receptionist—which could have suited a restricted person like me was the sole preserve of the white labour force and to a limited extent that of Coloured women too.

To put it succinctly the job adverts would state for "whites only" or "Coloureds only need apply." I was not deterred by the adverts for "Coloureds only" job category. I used to fool myself by imagining that "surely in any business a worker's proficiency should be the criterion."

At a local telephone booth I phoned the various offices for appointments and interviews. I gave the name Joyce only; if I had been white I would have been asked "Miss Joyce what?"

The interviews followed the normal pattern of filling a job application form on the spot. I always omitted filling the race classification because I wanted to

72

go through with the interview first. But the race specification was always the reason for the employer refusing me the job. "But I'm sorry we specifically stated in the advert that Coloured persons need only apply," an employer would say. Others would excuse themselves by declaring that their white workers would object, that it was against government policy, or that they had never employed a "Bantu" woman before. The job prospects were thus bleak even before I could bring in the obstacle of being a banned person. I would return to the location to face Nkosinathi's probing questions.

"Did you get the job Mom?"—"No," I would reply.

"Why do the Boers not give you a job?"—"It's because I am Black."

"But, you worked before you went to Pretoria."—"Well, those were clever Boers who had given me a job before."

"Why don't you go back to them then?"—"I can't. The shit buckets (meaning the Special Branch) banned me."

"What do they think we are going to eat?"—"They don't care a damn."

"We'll get them one day Mom."—"Oh, yes one of these days we'll get them."

Whiling away the time at number 7703 by emptying the ash and polishing my mother's Dover Coal stove made by Dormanlong of England revived painful memories of my sojourn in Pretoria Central where the bars of my cell door had been manufactured by the same company.

As I knelt scrubbing and polishing cold cement floors of the house a vivid picture of African women prisoners in uniform who did the same task at Pretoria Central recurred in my mind. The difference was I cleaned the house floors when necessary, but theirs was an ordeal. They had to shine the already sparkling floors as a punishment. In other ways I felt not much better off than I would have been in jail.

When, on one of those melancholic days, Barney Simons, a drama teacher and playwright, sent a message offering me a job, I was pleased. Ironically during the interview I was the one who asked him if he "was not afraid of getting into trouble with the police by employing me." It was arranged that I should have the job at Dorkay House, the cultural centre.

Having got the job I had to go and collect the "dompass." It was in the possession of the Special Branch officer who was in charge of my detention on the fateful day of May 12, 1969. I was required to report in person at the Special Branch Division of John Vorster Square where an officer would hand it over to me.

I must confess I feared for my life as I went up that computer-like manipulated lift to the ninth floor of the security division. I could hardly hear my own footsteps as I was led into the appropriate office. In the area, the atmosphere was gripped by the stillness found only at the crematorium.

The only words of the officer who handed me the "stinker" were that if I got myself into "mischief" again there would be no chance for me to answer back. I took the dompass.

When I landed on the streets a few seconds thereafter, I heaved a sigh of relief. There was John Vorster Square towering on me like a colossus. I moved away in haste. As I was safely crammed inside the coach of a train roaring back to Soweto, I tried to figure out just how on earth could detainees be reported as having jumped out of windows of the security side of JVS. It was impossible I said to myself. During those few minutes I was inside that section I spotted no window, though when viewing the building from outside there are windows to be seen. Are they perhaps shuttered inside, I asked myself.

On the following morning I got a friend to take my reference book to the *Mail* office for the endorsement of the date of my termination of duty. I waited in the street as my banning order prohibited me from entering the newspaper building. The following dawn I proceeded to the labour office where the same old procedure of job registration took place.

Dorkay House

Next day I arrived at Dorkay House. The apartheid padlock and its chain had been hanging over Dorkay House for some time when I reported for duty. To understand its plight it is necessary to briefly survey its history. Dorkay House is located in the neglected west end of Eloff Street, the busiest shopping precinct in Johannesburg. In its heyday it had been the mecca of progressive African arts, theatre workshops, and the school of Jazz and the Blues. Wasn't the famous musical "King Kong," which in the 1960's hit London's West End Theatres, a production of Dorkay House?

Dorkay House served as the stepping stone for talented singers like Miriam Makeba, Letta Mbuli and the Manhattan Brothers now of world acclaim. Some of those South African artists who today perform in British theatres and the BBC African productions, actors like Bloke Modisane and Lionel Ngakane made their debut at Dorkay House.

What delayed the complete shut down of Dorkay House was that during the 1950's and 1960's the apartheid machine concentrated their attack on political and trade union powerbases of the oppressed and the progressive forces. It thus gave a breathing space to institutions like Dorkay House which were involved in the cultural sphere.

By the 1970's it had succeeded in its first major task and now concentrated on the peripheral remnants not conforming to its ideology of apartheid. So now, when I set foot at Dorkay House in 1971, it was a hangover from the past cultural heritage.

There were two types of artists. Those who had made it in the past, but were now in decline because the true works of art were stifled by apartheid. Then

74

there were the younger and new artists who were full of verve, anger and excitement but now had no scope because of apartheid restrictions. The conflict of both groups was reminiscent of the divisive effects experienced by journalists soon after the Nationalist government came to power.

The bulk of the artists were Sowetonians. Dorkay House could not guarantee them permanent employment, so they had to obtain the daily labourer's permits whose limitations I described in the case of journalists. When working on a potentially successful production, the actors would receive weekly wages. But many of them had full-time jobs in the factories and rehearsed in the evenings. Those who relied on Dorkay House meagre wages were forever broke. I was also in charge of the petty-cash box and wages. It was normal practice to deduct every pay day, two thirds of an artist's wages to meet his petty cash debts.

Despite such problems there still remained progressive elements in Dorkay House. What the apartheid regime could not tolerate of institutions like Dorkay House was that you could find artists, directors, all and sundry sipping from the same cups and pouring from the same tea pot. Sometimes from the cubicle where I sat and typed I could hear artist and directors shouting at each other:

African voice—"What do you think I am, a garden boy?"

White voice—"What do you think I am, Vorster, your boss?"

At the time of my employment, a play entitled "Phiri" was in production. According to government regulations permits are to be applied for to stage a play be it before segregated audiences. When the company submitted the application it was told that permits would be issued on condition I got the sack.

So I lost my job. I did not put up a challenge. I felt it was not worth it. In Dorkay House itself there was another theatre company whose producers were blacks who to a certain extent did not want to have any dialogue with whites (though the company's trusteeship was of necessity in the hands of whites). One of its producers, Phineas Phetoe, produced a militant play portraying the armed struggle against white domination. It was incredible that the regime had given him a permit to stage the play. Phetoe was imbued with the Pan-African philosophy. He had travelled overseas and had set foot in Nigeria where he breathed the air of independence. On return home he desired "liberation" and he stopped consulting "whites."

For whatever reason the regime gave him an opportunity to air his views. When he "got too big for his boots" in his pursuance of the theatre of black liberation, the regime struck. He and some of his actors were detained under Section Six of the Terrorism Act.

Outside Dorkay House there were also "his master's voice" drama and music groups which received full backing and support from the state mass media. These were tribal groups like Mbaqanqa whose music was the ridicule of Sowetonians. "How can the Boers call sounds of a bellowing cow or a cock's crow, good music?" they would ask.

75

Then there were groups geared for the overseas entertainment. Sponsors of such groups had full government backing too. By adapting traditional dances and music to modern choreography and rhythm, they produced fantastic entertainment. The fallacy of it was that it mirrored the actors as not Sowetonians but as Bantustan bumpkins.

The true Sowetonian producer and artists were limited in depicting the social ills of the community. Their plays lacked any form of rebellion against poverty and oppression. When they did endeavour to portray the truth, the regime's censorship quickly fell on the production.

I faced the second stay at home period with a better frame of mind. I bought a second-hand electric typewriter with money Kenneth had sent me before. With it, I did odd typing jobs for various people. At the same time I taught myself knitting on a machine given to me by a friend.

The stay at home did not last long. I got a job cutting address stencils with an office of prospectors. It was a new business venture, whose Canadian director seemed not to understand what I was saying to him about having to submit my work address at the police station and that he should not be surprised when the Special Branch called. The branchmen did call. As the director told me later, "I assured them you will find yourself in the streets if you tried any tricks in my office." I did not need to try any tricks!

That office was clearly a new one without the obvious apartheid trappings. There was a common kitchen where everyone could make their own tea or coffee using the same utensils. However, with the appointment of a local white woman, things suddenly changed. She was openly hostile to the black staff and ordered that each member of it should make the tea in turn and that there should be separate facilities. When my turn came I refused, not having been employed to make tea. An altercation ensued, followed by a fracas. Police were called. On hearing the woman's hysterical allegations that I was a "commie," the police—who were the ordinary law enforcement officers—refused to act. The matter was referred to the Special Branch. When they left the office, I immediately went for legal advice and proceeded to lay a charge of assault against the woman, at John Vorster Square.

On the same evening, the security police arrived at home. They asked what had happened. To disarm them, I said I had taken legal advice and had laid a charge of assault against the woman. They left saying they would investigate the matter further. No further action followed.

From this bitter experience, it was apparent that chances for me, as a banned person, of staying permanently at any job were severely limited. Being at home again, I concentrated on knitting garments and selling them. The work was as unprofitable as my mother's home dressmaking. I could not enter adjacent locations to sell the garments. Moreover the political police were successful at harassing the boutique customers I supplied the knitwear to in the City.

Black Consciousness

During these times there emerged an unfamiliar type of nationalism espoused by black students throughout South Africa. It was termed "Black Consciousness." To understand what Black Consciousness was all about, it is important to analyse briefly the period in which it emerged and what were its strongest bases.

Black Consciousness was a variant nationalism as compared to the inclusive South African nationalism advocated by progressive forces like the African National Congress of South Africa and the exclusive African nationalism of the Pan-African Congress which rejected the inclusion of other racial groups. Champions of Black Consciousness were African, Indian and Coloured students who in their policy rejected "dialogue" with whites. Their slogan, coined by one of the movement's founder organisers, was "Black man you are on your own."

Black Consciousness was propagated by a generation of the oppressed youth which had been nurtured on apartheid from the moment their eyes opened on the world. Apartheid dictated to them in no uncertain terms that South Africa was for whites only and they, as blacks had no claim to it. Apartheid instilled in them that, as blacks, they were inferior to whites. And all this was done in the name of God and to preserve Western civilization.

During the time of open public political campaigns by progressive parties and the years when the apartheid regime was taking power, the majority of the Black Consciousness advocates were either unborn, in their nappies or toddlers. They were therefore not exposed to the campaigns of the political movements of the oppressed and other progressive forces.

By the early sixties, the apartheid regime had dealt devastating blows to all its political opponents. The leadership of such organisations as the ANC-SA, PAC and SACP (Communist Party) were either in jail or exile. Some were dead and some silenced by banning orders. The government banned the ANC of SA and PAC—the SACP had been proscribed earlier. The regime confiscated all available historical material of the people's struggles against tyranny. The banned organisations were faced with the difficult task of reconstruction in underground conditions. They had no easy access to the youth. Instead the government had the upper hand. It had control of the radio network. It created a watchdog to suppress the country's mass media. Above all it created a system of separate education for each racial group, which in the case of the Africans was down-graded to tribalism. It therefore forbade mixed universities and built segregated tribal universities.

In this situation the black youth found itself truly "on its own." It was completely exposed to fascist indoctrination which made its indelible mark on the youth's perspective. When the students' message for self-assertion and self-help by the black people as a group, accompanied by vociferous attacks on the "arrogant white liberals who think they can speak for us," the apartheid regime was the first to applaud. The white power elite which took offence were the opposition parties which referred to the students as "displaying ugly heads of rabid nationalism." In the meantime, the regime's mass media, especially the "Current Affairs" programme sang praises with an air of authority to the Black Consciousness slogan of "Black man you are on your own". It supported the attack on "liberals" whom it alleged were interfering in the political affairs of others.

In short, the government interpreted the Black Consciousness movement as a positive acceptance of its policy of separate development. It maintained the dogma that contact between black and white creates conflict, and at last "our proteges" have come to accept this crucial factor. So the black South African Students' Organisation (SASO) was encouraged.

By its interpretation the regime had made a preposterous error. The Black Consciousness movement swiftly reacted and dismissed such high-handed ovation by the "system." The movement was thus forced to come out clearly on the political plane. It immediately launched an attack on the system's philosophy of separate development. The Bantustan creation was vociferously attacked. The Bantustan chiefs—men like Kaiser Mantanzima and Gatsha Buthelezi—were called puppets of the Vorster government. The regime staged a retreat.

Adult people of the working class communities like Soweto received the youth's message with cautious understanding. Parents understood full well the reasons behind their children's gospel. But it would be a folly to assume that as workers they felt closely drawn into it.

Black underground activists conceded the need for an overground resistance movement. It successfully illustrated that, despite two decades of apartheid rule, black people rejected white domination. As expected, the movement was deplorably lacking in history, politics and economics. "The SASO boys will learn" the underground activists asserted. It became of paramount importance for experienced activists to share their knowledge and experience with selected members of the movement.

Many underground activists endeavoured to do such political work. But no sooner had the Black Consciousness started talking about creating conditions for the formation of a broad political movement and supporting the trade union efforts, than the apartheid regime struck with an iron hand. It banned the movement's leadership, removing some of it from the urban areas. As each generation grows up, however, it is motivated to continue the struggle, mainly through the student groups. The events of 1976 showed this clearly.

Into Exile

By 1973 I had come to the decision that I had, after all, to leave South Africa. The government was making new threats that it was going to take firm action against what it termed "political agitators" working in the black communities.

78

It looked to me as if I was destined for another spell of internment. I now had two children, Nkosinathi, who was seven, and a baby daughter born in January 1973. She had been born on a Monday. That Sunday evening the labour pains started. Under the terms of my banning order I was required to report to the local police station every Monday morning. My mother was worried, and wanted to telephone the police from a call box to tell them I would not be able to report —otherwise they would come and arrest me, and my new-born infant. I refused to let her telephone, because there is a limit to the human degradation anyone should suffer.

During labour, the midwife on rota duty pleaded with me to go by jeep to the clinic so she could attend all the night cases together. "Daughter of the soil," she said "you understand how short-staffed we are." I agreed to go. Night deliveries at the clinic, which is not equipped for obstetric cases, were done without the knowledge of the white authorities who were safely off at home. All those in labour that night were collected by jeep, and there we were, five women lying on ordinary stretchers covered by rubber sheets and newspapers. The room was cold. After she was born Nomzamo cried distressingly for a long time. At 5 a.m. we were led back into the jeep and dropped off at our homes, while the clinic was tidied up for the white staff arriving for duty. Two of the mothers taken home were still in an advanced stage of labour.

Because of the threatened clamp-down, I felt I had to choose between leaving the children for another spell of internment, or leaving them behind while I left the country and then make arrangements to have them re-united with me. So in July 1973 in a carefully planned escape I left the country to join the national liberation movement in exile. As only destiny could have arranged, while I was in Zambia I met Kenneth again. But it was two years since I had written to him, and more than four since I had seen him. And I was now an angry woman full of revolutionary fight directed against the apartheid state. However, there was plenty of time to reflect on what had happened between the two of us. In the end we decided to get married. We now have a son of our own, Samora, an adopted son Vikela and we are working on plans for Nkosinathi and Nomzamo to join our family—and then we hope to return to Africa.

Since I left South Africa and indeed since I started writing this book, Soweto has hit the headlines of the world. As a result of the violent police reaction to the school students' demonstrations Soweto, already a dangerous place, has become positively fatal for youth. Many students and children have been killed at random and hundreds have been rounded up and detained.

Conditions of living have undoubtedly deteriorated. The government in Pretoria announced some well-publicised "concessions" such as the official withdrawal of Afrikaans in schools and the re-introduction of house ownership on 30-year leases. But these are verbal concessions only, not having the force of law. Soweto is governed directly by proclamation. Anyway, where is the average Sowetonian to get the money to buy his little home? He still earns starvation wages, prices are rising all the time, transport costs and food for the family have to be paid. Moreover, all the concessions can be made null and void by the insistence of the authorities that Soweto residents take out "Bantustan citizenship" before they apply for leases, passports etc. Just now Sowetonians with Xhosa names are being made to take pass books stamped with "T" for Transkei. And in March 1977 the Government announced the doubling of fines for pass law "offences." These are the crucial matters, not "concessions" announced to fool the overseas market.

There is no improvement in the ghettoes of South Africa and no progress until the whole apartheid system is removed.

Printed by A. G. Bishop & Sons Ltd., Orpington, Kent.